WINNING AT FOLLOWING

WINNING AT FOLLOWING

Secrets to Success in Supporting Roles

J. NORMAN BALDWIN

 PRAEGER™

An Imprint of ABC-CLIO, LLC
Santa Barbara, California • Denver, Colorado

Library of Congress Cataloging-in-Publication Data

Names: Baldwin, J. Norman, author.
Title: Winning at following : secrets to success in supporting roles / J.
    Norman Baldwin.
Description: Santa Barbara, California : Praeger, [2017] | Includes
    bibliographical references and index.
Identifiers: LCCN 2016049064 | ISBN 9781440853142 (hardcopy : alk. paper) |
    ISBN 9781440853159 (eBook)
Subjects: LCSH: Followership.
Classification: LCC HD57.8 .B35 2017 | DDC 650.1—dc23
LC record available at https://lccn.loc.gov/2016049064

ISBN: 978-1-4408-5314-2
EISBN: 978-1-4408-5315-9

21 20 19 18 17   1 2 3 4 5

This book is also available as an eBook.

Praeger
An Imprint of ABC-CLIO, LLC

ABC-CLIO, LLC
130 Cremona Drive, P.O. Box 1911
Santa Barbara, California 93116-1911
www.abc-clio.com

This book is printed on acid-free paper ∞

Manufactured in the United States of America

For
Joe, Gillie, Susan, and Matthew

Contents

Preface

The Motivation for and Purpose of This Book

I am going to visit with you about the most common, yet underrated and overlooked role that we play in life—the role of follower. Although we are *all* followers in many capacities in our lives, follower ranks a distant last as a popular topic in the research and writing on the dozen most common roles that we play in life—parent, mother, father, sister, brother, friend, leader, manager, employee, teacher, and student (see table 1).[1] This ranking is particularly alarming in light of the amount of time—an average of 47 hours a week—that most of us spend functioning as followers in work environments.[2] But more importantly, the scant attention to the role of follower in work environments is especially disturbing given the significance of followership in determining our wages and work conditions. When the boss is pleased with our followership, we position ourselves for pay raises, promotions, and job assignments that enhance our standard of living and quality of work life. When the boss is disappointed, we jeopardize our job security, fail to earn pay raises that maintain our standard of living, and frequently relegate ourselves to the least appealing assignments in our work environments. So, instead of addressing how to be a great leader, the most common topic in the management literature and research, *Winning at Following* addresses how to be a great follower, a road less traveled that, ironically, affects far greater numbers of people than the millions of epistles directed at the few who are leaders.

However, the intention of this book goes beyond merely reporting the qualities of ideal followers that are found in the academic literature. Developing these qualities may garner rewards from appreciative bosses,

Table 1 Frequency that Common Roles Appear in the Titles of Books and Articles

Role	Citations	Role	Citations
Student	5,671,685	Manager	1,024,744
Leader	3,165,183	Employee	995,412
Teacher	2,266,092	Father	822,678
Parent	1,535,810	Brother	790,713
Mother	1,399,144	Follower	48,045
Friend	1,315,873		

Source: EBSCO Discovery Service, accessed January 19, 2015.

but this does not guarantee a happy and satisfied follower. *Winning at Following*, consequently, endeavors to reveal the organizational environments that are most compatible with your natural followership style. Moreover, the book reviews the research on the most appealing jobs for followers and reports the findings from the academic research on work-related factors that will bring you job satisfaction as a follower. Although full of research findings that provide fact-based instructions on how to succeed in follower roles, you do not need to be an academic to read this book. *Winning at Following* communicates its messages in a down-to-earth style and is replete with stories that illustrate its major themes.

Chapter–by-Chapter Overview

Taking an axe to the pedestal on which our culture places leaders and the study of leadership, the central thesis of the first chapter is that leadership is an overrated and often unappealing role in contemporary organizations. The chapter begins by recognizing our romance with leadership by documenting the enormous volume of writings on leadership relative to the writings on followership. It then proceeds to demonstrate that executive-level leadership roles characterized by high pay and status are *not* attractive jobs for a lot of people. The sobering realities of executive-level leadership positons are revealed through the story of my nephew's experience as the head football coach at the University of Tennessee. In the second half of the chapter, the curricula from the leading Executive Master of Business Administration (EMBA) programs in the country are presented with the intent of demonstrating that the requisite skills for effective contemporary executive leaders are diverse and likely to bore a lot of people.

The drawbacks of leadership presented in chapter 1 set the stage for the virtues of followership presented in chapter 2. In contrast to leaders, followers avoid rising to their level of incompetence, resolving a continual onslaught of petty employee conflicts, and enduring an unremitting torrent of employee complaints about their assignments, performance evaluations, pay raises, work conditions, and hurt feelings.[3] I next address the tremendous power that followers can exercise as informal leaders without having to maneuver through the snake pits that are the responsibility of the formal leader.

For those of you looking for authoritative direction on what you need to do in order to be an outstanding follower, you need to look no further than chapter 3. This chapter presents findings from 53 articles and books that prescribe the 375 ideal traits, skills, and behaviors of followers. These accounts identify three main skills or characteristics of ideal followers. Ideal followers are *active*, *effective communicators*, and *interpersonally skillful*. Second-tier qualities that surface from the findings of the larger and most methodologically rigorous studies are also identified.

Since developing ideal follower qualities can be challenging, chapter 4 provides instructions on how to bring about change in your life. In short, this chapter endeavors to teach you how to change habits in order to become a more highly valued follower.

Chapter 5 assumes that some of you may not be able to realize the qualities of the ideal follower, so your best option is to find organizational environments that fit your given followership style. The chapter begins by presenting the findings from 20 articles and books that identify 90 different followership types. Because they overlap, the follower types are reduced to five dichotomous categories: active versus passive, conforming versus individualistic, committed versus alienated, pragmatic versus idealistic, and self-oriented versus altruistic. The chapter culminates in a test to determine your followership type.

Chapters 6 and 7 identify the organizational leadership styles, cultures, and climates that are compatible and incompatible with your followership style. Chapter 8, in turn, presents the results of the research that identifies the factors that predict follower job satisfaction. Chapter 9 next reviews the studies that identify the best and worst jobs for followers. Many of the findings are quite surprising. For example, who would guess that being a dental hygienist is one of the top ten best jobs in America, while being a newspaper reporter is among the top ten worst jobs? The underlying assumption of chapters 8 and 9 is that you win at following through working in jobs that bring you satisfaction and fulfillment, pay well, and offer job security and a promising future.

Chapters 10 and 11 make the case that, through becoming skillful at overcoming common serious problems in organizations, you can greatly enhance your capacity to win at following. The bulk of chapters 10 and 11 provides practical advice to followers on how to pass on bad news to superiors and how to deal with micromanaging bosses, unethical superiors, sexual harassers, and abusive, bullying bosses.

Chapter 12 concludes the book by revisiting the central themes leading to winning at following. The themes emphasize the dual nature of winning through becoming not just a more proficient follower, but also a more satisfied and fulfilled follower. I conclude the book by telling stories about three friends and a family member who are often followers, yet, through their character, willpower, and benevolence, they have an extraordinary impact on the lives of others that epitomizes the exercise of true leadership masquerading as the follower's role.

Acknowledgments

No book is conceived, completed, and refined for publication without the contributions and inspiration of others. I would like to thank the community of scholars who write on followership, especially Robert Kelley, Ira Chaleff, and Barbara Kellerman for their seminal works that have legitimized the study of followership and elevated awareness of the significance of the roles of followers in contemporary organizations. I would also like to thank George Thompson, director of the Publisher-in-Residence Program at The University of Alabama (UA), and my literary agent, Stan Wakefield, for their sage insights and supportive spirits that gave me the confidence to proceed with this manuscript. Plus, I give special thanks to the highest performing undergraduate that I have ever taught, Emily Scheiner, for her invaluable contribution to the research for chapter 10 and to an outstanding couple—Paul and Karen Lashley—who provided a superb job critiquing and editing the book. Finally, beyond the extraordinary friends and family to whom I dedicate this manuscript, I appreciate beyond words the selfless contributions of my wife to this book. Without Karen's gifts of wisdom and insight, as well as her critical eye for detail, this book would never be worthy of an editor's nod of approval, neither would you the reader ever see the ink on paper of this concluding sentence of the preface.

CHAPTER 1

Leadership: Everyone's
Fair-Haired Child

In the bliss of childhood, we dream of stardom on the stage, greatness on the gridiron, and glory on the battlefield. In time, we learn about institutions that propel our youthful imaginations in new directions and toward ambitions that may embrace the operating room, Congress, the courthouse, and even the White House. But with every year of maturation, the world becomes a little larger, the evaluations of our talent become more frequent, and failure to be selected becomes a more common experience. Our first great humbling experience befalls all of us the moment we begin grammar school. Beyond the insularity of our homes and neighborhoods, the random odds of leading the class scholastically, being elected to student council, landing the lead in the class play, or winning the class dodgeball competition lowers to 1 in 21.2—the average number of students in an elementary school class.[1] Meanwhile, the sobriety that begins in childhood is pitted against a media that resurrects our intoxicating dreams of grandeur through a constant deluge of tales, myths, and true stories of great leaders and superheroes. Moreover, even the sacred halls of academia are a guilty party to this large-scale seduction of our egos and aspirations.

Leadership—Our Romance with an Overrated Role

Armed with their doctorates and scientific methods of inquiry, scholars cannot resist the allure and romance of studying and writing about leadership. Since the beginning of the 21st century, ABI Inform Complete, the leading search engine for business-related literature, reports 6,660 scholarly, peer-reviewed journal articles with the word "leadership" in their titles and only 21 similar articles with the word "followership" in their titles.[2] For every scholarly article on followership, 293 articles exist on leadership. Broadening the search to include both peer-reviewed publications and nonacademic publications[3] and utilizing a search engine that captures the literature in almost every academic discipline reveals 633,625 articles published in the 21st century with "leadership" in their titles and only 958 articles with "followership" in their titles—a ratio of 661.4 to 1.[4] But get this, a search for leadership- and followership-related publications available through the Library of Congress, the largest library in the United States and the second largest library in the world, reveals 268,851 leadership-related publications and only 64 publications related to followership—a ratio of 4,200 to 1.[5]

The extraordinary abilities and accomplishments of famous leaders fascinate us. At age 61 and weighing only 99 pounds, Mahatma Gandhi led a 241-mile march in protest of an unreasonable British tax on salt.[6] Theodore Roosevelt insisted on giving a lengthy campaign speech after being shot by a bullet that lodged a quarter of an inch from his heart.[7] And, Nelson Mandela spent 27 years in prison, including 13 years of sunup-to-sundown hard labor in a limestone quarry and 18 years of living in an eight-by-seven-foot cell without a bed or toilet.[8] The unique physical shortcomings and quirky habits of famous leaders also capture our imaginations. Alexander the Great was rumored to have one brown eye and one blue eye, Steve Jobs claimed he needed to bathe only once a week because he was a fruitarian, and former British Prime Minister David Cameron gives his important speeches with a full bladder to enhance his focus.[9]

For those of you who aspire to be leaders, biographies and autobiographies of great people also help us to learn the character qualities and behaviors that are instrumental for becoming a leader. And yes, would it not be terrific to become a huge leadership success and enjoy the status, admiration, and life style of a Bill Gates, Condoleezza Rice, or Nick Saban?

But is the study of leadership and great leaders really as significant as the volumes of literature on these topics? As someone who began teaching about leadership at the graduate level in 1981, my answer is no. Americans, including those in academia, have inflated perceptions of the role of leaders in the successful operation of organizations in all sectors of our culture. Leadership is like that enchantingly handsome boyfriend or that beautiful, beguiling girlfriend who we cannot resist but who fails to live up to our expectations for a meaningful and constructive relationship.

To drive my point home further, let me emphasize what I repeatedly learned in my PhD program. I was indelibly taught to act like a physician when addressing the health and well-being of organizations. Like a physician, one gathers and analyzes all sorts of information, renders a diagnosis, and then prescribes treatments (solutions) to what ails an organization. Given the myriad of potential causes of an organizational problem, the odds do not favor leadership being identified as center stage. Off the top of my head, here are ten quick *other problem areas* in the internal environment of organizations that are just as likely to be the culprit: production technology, organization structure, operations and procedures, finance and accounting systems, job designs, compensation systems, strategic plans, communication systems, employee skill levels, and red tape. Yet the buck stops at the top, as leaders routinely lose their jobs when the cause of a problem may actually be occurring four or five levels below their daily responsibilities and operational purview.

When leadership is defined or structured around the idea of *one* person leading an organization, the elevated significance of leadership seems even more preposterous in 21st-century developed countries. Given contemporary emphasis on power sharing and decentralized decision-making in an increasingly democratic world, there are typically more checks and balances on a leader's independent power than ever before. Moreover, ascribing the success of an organization to a leader is like giving the credit for the Chicago Bulls' six NBA championships and dual "three-peats" in eight years to Phil Jackson without recognizing the significance of the cast of players, including the great Michael Jordan. Unfortunately, the heroic leader, a well-embedded romantic concept in our culture, is much easier to understand than the operations of "complex systems of multi-level networks" and a myriad of variables in the internal and external environments of an organization.[10]

After arriving at the belief that leadership is overrated and followership underrated, I was pleased to learn that I am not alone, but in fact, in good company. Barbara Kellerman, the James McGregor Burns Lecturer in Public Leadership at Harvard's Kennedy School of Government contends, "To fixate on leaders at the expense of followers is misguided, even mistaken. The latter are every bit as consequential as the former."[11] James Rosenau, professor of International Affairs at George Washington University further asserts that human beings "tend to exaggerate the importance of leaders and downplay their own role. . . . Followership is of such importance that often it is not clear who is leading and who is following."[12] However, the father figure of the study of followership, Robert Kelley, a professor in the Tepper School of Business at Carnegie Mellon University, makes the strongest statement about the significance of followership in asserting, "Leaders contribute on average no more than 20% to the success of most organization. . . . Followers are critical to the remaining 80%."[13]

Leadership—the Dream Disguising a Nightmare

In 2002, I had the honor of serving as the president of the Faculty Senate at The University of Alabama. In running a 50-person Senate and a 17-person steering committee and advocating for over 1,100 faculty members, I contend that I had the third most demanding job on campus next to the jobs of the university president and the provost. Although I knew the job would be challenging, little did I know that my e-mail messages would triple and that seemingly no one on campus understood that you do not initiate problem-solving by starting at the top. Instead of a leader, I realized that I was predominantly a clearinghouse—a glorified operator or the faculty's live directory—that referred everyone to where they should have started with their problems in the first place! To get any real work done, I had to wait until everyone else's workday was done. And yes, the faculty senate ended up addressing important issues. We tried to racially integrate the Greek system on campus, fought for domestic partner benefits for university employees, created a system of 360-degree feedback for deans and department chairs, and developed a model ombudsperson system.

Yet, in the end, we failed to achieve many of our goals and in the process, managed to peeve a lot of important people, as well as a lot of unimportant but doggedly mean-spirited people. However, I rationalized that all of the hard work and the invective that I experienced did not matter because I knew that, at the end of the workday, I could go home to what really mattered—a wife who loved me unconditionally and stood by me through thick and thin. Well, wrong. I do have a wonderful wife, but it was clear around halfway through my term as senate president, that if I was going to stay on for another term, I would likely be doing so as a single man unless I controlled my work-related foul moods. But more relevant to the intent of this book, my experience as president of the Faculty Senate at UA taught me what many former leaders know. Although the idea of being a leader is seductive and the status and attention that come with it are intoxicating, working in a prestigious leadership position is a putrid job for a lot of people.

Take my nephew, Derek Dooley, who served as a head football coach for six years at Louisiana Tech University and the University of Tennessee. Derek is the son of the legendary Vince Dooley, the former head coach of The University of Georgia (UGA) who coached at UGA from 1964 to 1988 and won a national championship in 1980. Based on his academics, Derek was admitted to the University of Virginia (UVA), arguably the finest state university in the South. At UVA, he walked onto the football team his freshman year and earned an athletic scholarship at the end of his sophomore year. By his senior year, he earned a position in the starting lineup as a wide receiver. From UVA, Derek returned home to earn a law degree from UGA and proceeded to take a job with Nelson Mullins Riley & Scarborough, a law firm in Atlanta, in 1994.

After only two years in his law practice, Derek decided to trade in his law books and Brooks Brothers suits for sweatshirts and cleats. He was going to become a football coach and was willing to start at the bottom. He joined the UGA football program as a graduate assistant earning a fraction of the salary he had earned as an attorney.

UGA's defensive coordinator, Joe Kines, described Derek as a sponge for his capacity to absorb the football knowledge necessary for coaching. By the time his assistantship was completed, armed with an arsenal of football knowledge and the Dooley name, Derek was primed to land his first collegiate coaching job, which was offered by Mike Cavan, the head coach of Southern Methodist University (SMU).

Mike Cavan was Vince Dooley's starting quarterback who led the Georgia Bulldogs to the 1968 Sugar Bowl appearance that most Bulldog fans would like to forget. Like Derek, Mike Cavan was a pretty boy with Southern savoir faire. Paired with Derek, they were double trouble when they set out to charm the mom of any prize recruit. More importantly, as a follower of Mike Cavan, Derek learned how to be a wide receivers coach and a recruiting coordinator.

After three seasons at SMU, Derek was ready to jump to the next level and managed to hook a big fish, or perhaps better said, a big fisherman hooked him. In 2000, Nick Saban, the new head coach at Louisiana State University (LSU) and a man on the road to becoming the most successful college football coach of the 21st century, hired Derek as his recruiting coordinator and tight ends coach. Teamed with Saban, Derek eventually became LSU's running backs coach and special teams coordinator. In 2003, LSU won the BCS National Championship by defeating the University of Oklahoma 21 to 14 in the 2004 Nokia Sugar Bowl. As the recruiting coordinator, Derek played a central role in signing the junior and senior players who led the way. Following his mentor to the National Football League, Derek became the tight ends coach for the Miami Dolphins for a short two-year stint. After ten years of apprenticeship and following, Derek secured his first job as a head coach at Louisiana Tech in Rustin, Louisiana. Three years later, he arrived—Derek snagged a career destination job, as he became the 22nd head coach of the University of Tennessee Volunteers in 2010.

Coming from a family with 13 relatives who have played Division I college football, there is no telling how many thousands of football games my family members have watched. If you were to ask any of us who the unluckiest football player or coach in the family is, you would find a unanimous answer—Derek Dooley as head coach of UT. In Derek's first season, Tennessee began a victory celebration and trip to the locker room as UT beat the number 10 ranked LSU Bengal Tigers in Baton Rouge by a score of 14 to 10. But before he made it to the locker room, the officials ushered Derek back to the sidelines. Tennessee had too many players on the field for the final play of the game, and the rules prevented the game from ending on a penalty. With zero seconds remaining on the clock, LSU running back Stevan Ridley rammed his way over left tackle to steal the win in what became dubbed as the "Miracle Victory."[14]

Appearing in the Music City Bowl at the end of Derek's first season, Tennessee had beaten the University of North Carolina by a score of 20–17. The Tar Heels had advanced the ball to the Tennessee 16-yard line, but T. J. Yates, the Tar Heels' quarterback, failed to spike the ball in time for a game-tying field goal. The referee announced the end of the game, players streamed to the middle of the field in celebration, and the coaches completed the obligatory end-of-the-game handshake. However, the replay official called for a review of the last play of the game and declared that one second remained on the clock. Returned to the sideline for one last play, Derek watched North Carolina placekicker Casey Barth launch a successful field goal to send the game into overtime. Still tied going into the second overtime, Tennessee quarterback Tyler Bray drilled a completion to Quan Sturdivant. Unfortunately, Quan was a UNC linebacker. Casey Barth returned to the field to kick a 23-yard field goal to steal another painful win from Tennessee and its first-year coach.

The poster child for bad things that can happen in a football game, Derek stepped down as the head football coach of the University of Tennessee on November 18, 2012. His storybook ascension to an elite head coaching job came to an end. However, there is a silver lining to Derek's story.

Derek is now working in a follower's role. His work responsibilities are more manageable, he has more time for his family, and he can leave the pressures of his job at work. He gets paid well and has the status of coaching wide receivers for the most highly financially valued football team in the NFL—the Dallas Cowboys.[15] By contrast, as head coach of the Tennessee Volunteers, he was the CEO for 112 players, 10 assistant coaches, and around 28 staff and graduate assistants who reported directly to him.[16] During the season, in addition to overseeing *all* operations of the football team, he was tasked with coaching special teams, speaking at five press conferences per week, and appearing weekly on a television and radio show.[17] In the off-season, additional burdens included leading a football marketing campaign, giving 20 to 30 speeches, participating in fundraising, and playing the central role in recruiting prize athletes. Year-round, he played psychologist to malcontented players, parents of players, wealthy donors, and know-it-all football fans who have no idea what it takes to revive a football program in an incredibly competitive conference in Division I college football. Given the incessant coverage of college football in contemporary social media, Derek could never escape the weight of being a head football coach. He was under the microscope day and night. He is now a free man.

Executive Jobs: Candy for Some, Caster Oil for Others

If the responsibilities of a head football coach still appeal to you, let's take a look at what executives do more broadly speaking. First, I must acknowledge that the ideal skill set for executive leadership is going to vary from organization to organization based on a host of factors—you do not run Google or Disney World the same way you run Mary Kay or the New York Yankees. However, the required core courses in the curriculums of leading Executive Master of Business Administration (EMBA) programs provide a general idea of the knowledge areas that leading scholars believe are essential for shaping the thinking and behavior of executives. So, what kind of training do the following top-ranked EMBA programs offer?[18]

- Anderson School of Business, University of California, Los Angeles[19]
- Booth School of Business, University of Chicago[20]
- Fuqua School of Business, Duke University[21]
- Kellogg School of Management, Northwestern University[22]
- Wharton School of Business, the University of Pennsylvania[23]

Table 1.1 reveals seven skill areas in which top-ranked EMBA programs in the country are training current and aspiring executives. Moreover,

Table 1.1   Skill Areas and Core Course Work in the Five-Leading Executive Master of Business Administration Programs in America

Skill Area	Course Titles	Total Courses in the Skill Area
Finance and Accounting	1. Advanced Financial Policy for Management 2. Corporate Finance (2)[a] 3. Financial Policy for Managers 4. Financial Reporting Systems 5. Financial Strategy 6. Global Financial Management 7. Financial Accounting (4) 8. Managerial Accounting (2)	13
Strategy	1. Advanced Marketing Strategy[b] 2. Competitive Strategy & Business Policy 3. Corporate Strategy 4. Financial Strategy[b] 5. Foundations for Strategy Formulation (2) 6. Global Strategy & Economics[b] 7. Managing the Productive Core: Operations Strategy[b] 8. Marketing Strategy & Policy[b] 9. Marketing Strategy[b] 10. Strategic Leadership[b] 11. Strategic Management Research	12
Leadership	1. Essentials of Leadership 2. Foundations of Teamwork and Leadership 3. Integrative Leadership Experience I and II 4. Leadership and Development 5. Leadership and Organizations 6. Leadership Exploration and Development 7. Leadership Foundation I, II, and III 8. Leadership, Ethics, and Organization 9. Strategic Leadership[b]	11

Skill Area	Course Titles	Total Courses in the Skill Area
Statistics	1. Statistical Decision Analysis 2. Statistics Regression 3. Analysis for Business 4. Data Analysis & Management Decisions 5. Decision Modules	5
Operations Management	1. Operations Management (4) 2. Managing the Productive Core: Operations Strategy[b]	5
Microeconomics	1. Managerial Economics (2) 2. Microeconomics 3. Microeconomics for Managers 4. Economic Analysis for Managers	5
Macroeconomics	1. Macroeconomics 2. Macroeconomics and Global Economic Development 3. Macroeconomics & Economic Forecasting 4. Global Strategy & Economics[b]	4
Random Core Courses	1. Analytical Approach to Uncertainty 2. International Business Seminar 3. Management Communication 4. Managerial Decision Making 5. Managing the Enterprise 6. Management of Human Resources 7. Managing the Productive Core: Quality and Productivity 8. Managing the Productive Core: Business Analytics 9. Negotiations 10. Organizations and Incentives 11. Program Company Launch 12. Responsibility in Global Management	12

[a]Numbers in parentheses indicate the number of courses with the same title.
[b]Course is counted in more than one skill area.
Source: See endnotes 18, 19, 20, 21, and 22.

the average number of required courses, excluding elective courses, is 15. (These are typically three semester-hour courses.) Developing eight areas of core competencies through 15 required courses reflects a diverse body of preparatory training for executive-level leadership. Does a diverse education in preparation for a multifaceted job entice you? Take a look at the skill areas and specific course titles, and reflect on whether the curriculum is seductive enough to chart your ambition on a course toward an executive office. I find course work on strategy and leadership to be very enticing; plus, I could tolerate developing skills in marketing and macroeconomics. Operations management and statistics, however, scare me, and I would rather walk 10 miles to work with broken glass in my shoes than take course work in microeconomics or accounting. Ultimately, I must conclude that I am not the ideal student for an EMBA program and likely not a good fit for an executive-level job. If you are unsure of how you feel about the EMBA curriculums, then try to answer the following seemingly non sequitur question for fun: If you were a dog, what breed would you be?

What Kind of Dog Are You?

Several years ago, every family in my neighborhood seemed to be adding a dog to their household. I joined in on the canine frenzy by staying true to what academic nerds do—instead of purchasing a dog, I purchased five books on dogs. At the time, I was teaching a graduate course in public personnel administration and another in how to organize and manage government employees. To my surprise, in the process of reading these books, I had a minor epiphany—understanding the nature and behavior of dogs helped me better understand the nature and behavior of *Homo sapiens* in groups and organizations. Like dogs, human beings have genetic predispositions to be dominant or submissive, friendly or antisocial, territorial or inclusive, active or passive, and vigorous or gentle.[24]

Now, look at the two different lists of popular canines in table 1.2 and identify which list of dogs your personality and temperament are most like. Do not pick the category of dogs that you *like*, but again, pick the category that is *similar* to you.

If you identified with either the large or the small dogs in category A, you have revealed something potentially relevant to your capacity for leadership. If, for example, you are like a bloodhound, German shepherd, or shih tzu, you likely demonstrate a high level of behavioral constancy or tendency to engage in a limited number of highly focused

Table 1.2 Dogs with Similar Dispositions

Disposition A	Disposition B
Large Dogs A	**Large Dogs B**
Bloodhound	Boxer
Coonhound (Black and Tan)	Brittany Spaniel
Bulldog	Dalmatian
German Shepherd	English Setter
Great Dane	Golden Retriever
Siberian Husky	Irish Setter
Rottweiler	
St. Bernard	**Small Dogs B**
Schnauzer	Chihuahua
	Cocker Spaniel
Small Dogs A	Dachshund
Pug	Toy Poodle
Shih Tzu	

Source: Daniel F. Tortora, *The Right Dog for You* (New York: Simon and Schuster, 1980).

activities. Like the bloodhound or coonhound following the scent of a fox, you are not easily distracted. For example, on the weekends, when relaxed and free of household chores or yard work, you are likely to be engrossed in one or two hobbies that you cannot put down. On vacation, you prefer travelling to the same place every year or love having the freedom to immerse yourself in the same activity every summer. You fish, you golf, or you mountain bike, but you do not do all three.

If you are a column-A bloodhound-type employee, you can achieve tremendous professional success in jobs that capture your imagination sufficiently to sustain your unshakable capacity for focus. But, unfortunately, the odds favor that many of the diverse activities of leadership positions will likely bore you, or specific areas of leadership responsibility will captivate your enormous capacity for focus to the neglect of other significant responsibilities. If you are a column-A employee, you should not be the governor of your state or the CEO of a company. You should be the governor's expert on immigration policy, economic development, or social welfare policy or the company's expert on new product development, sales, or marketing. Ultimately, you should work in a job that genuinely interests you and that is sufficiently focused to allow you a sense of mastery and accomplishment that often cannot be achieved in performing the numerous, diverse roles of an executive.

If you identify with the canines in column B, you demonstrate lower levels of behavioral consistency and tend to delight in engaging in a variety of activities. Like the golden retriever and cocker spaniel, you like all sorts of people, and unlike the bloodhound, your foxhunt is long and nonlinear because it is full of intriguing side attractions. If you are more like the canine companions in column B, your weekend activities are varied and fluid. You enjoy playing golf or tennis, but you do not want either sport to be a weekend constant, and much of what you do is spontaneous or evolves as the weekend progresses. Column-B gals and guys take different vacations every summer and are more inclined to pack in a myriad of activities while on vacation. They do not want to take just a fishing vacation. While a vacation to the beach may include deep-sea fishing, it may also include waterskiing, windsurfing, beach volleyball, and crabbing.

The column-B person is much more inclined to enjoy the variety of activities characteristic of executive leadership positions. Moreover, column-B leaders are in a better position to tolerate and work within the unpredictable environments common in many 21st-century organizations. Given that executives are frequently at the epicenter of action during crises and times of rapid change, the boss who is like a golden retriever will often thrive under such circumstances. However, enjoying the variety of work of an executive-level leader does not guarantee success, especially if executives are distracted to the point of not being able to bring a project to closure.

Bill Clinton is an excellent example of a golden retriever leader who had an affinity for all sorts of people and loved the world of diverse policy ideas. His staff repeatedly immersed itself in developing new programs and policies only to have them aborted at the whim of President Clinton's appetite for the policy du jour.[25] Without the ability of Leon Panetta, Clinton's chief of staff, to bridle the president's impulses, enforce order in his meetings, and control who had access to the president, Clinton's presidency might likely be remembered for only two Ls—his libido and lackluster political performance. Ultimately, successful executive-level leaders lean toward the personality of the dogs in column B, but to ensure their success, they must be an even more selective breed of people. They should be able to control their impulse to veer from chosen paths, or they should be placed in situations where people, policy, or structure rein in their impulsiveness.

Conclusion: Be Careful What You Wish For at Work

The pathway to major leadership roles accompanied with fame and fortune is such a lengthy obstacle course full of roadblocks, potholes, poor maps, and misleading signposts that even the most highly ambitious people may never realize their biggest dreams. Moreover, when leadership dreams are realized, they can readily become leadership nightmares, as leadership roles are often recipes for misery for those with narrow, hound-dog interests; limited dimensions to their talents; thin skins; nine-to-five commitments to work, or overly compromised values. Bigtime leadership roles are for people who have boundless energy and time, varied talents, and dispositions that take delight in diverse and demanding responsibilities that are high impact, highly visible, and mercilessly scrutinized.

This book, however, is not about how to be an effective leader; it is about what almost every one of us is inside and outside of work. Whether we like it or not, we are followers. In the next chapter, we come to grips with this reality and look candidly at the vices and virtues of followership.

CHAPTER 2

Followership: The Undisputed Leader of Underrated Roles

Leader, Less Likely: Follower, Fact

Over the years, I have taught a lot of political science majors and always get a kick out of students who break down and share their desire to become the governor of Alabama, a U.S. senator, or a mayor of a city. I get an even bigger kick when they cockily say they "will be" a governor, senator, or mayor. Yet the biggest kick comes from when they actually make it.

But how did they make it to the top, and what were the odds of such a successful ride? The common recipe for leadership stardom typically includes extraordinary talent, hard work, and laser-like focus on goals. The formula also frequently includes being born into a privileged family and some fairy dust of good luck.

I have taught over 6,000 students in my career, including many who have been enormously successful in their careers, but I can think of two who made it to the top of their profession. One became the state's finance director and the head of the Alabama Education Association, and the other became the executive director of the Republican Party in Alabama. Given that one in nine workers is self-employed, one could contend that the self-employed are at the top of their professions, but that still leaves the overwhelming majority of employees as followers.[1]

Moreover, Joseph Rost, a professor emeritus of leadership studies at the University of San Diego, contends, "The number of leadership activities in the typical day in any organization is minimal for the large majority of people. . . . In a typical twenty-four hour period, how many people in the numerous nations of the world are actually engaged in activities intending significant change [a criterion for leadership]? The answer, I believe, is few."[2] In fact, Robert Kelley, the guru of follower-ship studies, maintains, "For most of us, followership represents 70 to 90 percent of our working days."[3]

Even those who assert that they are leaders are still followers in that they are accountable to stakeholders who can limit their power, dock their pay, or remove them from their positions. A CEO has to please shareholders and the board of directors, and even the president of the United States can be vetoed by Congress, be impeached by the House of Representatives, have his appointments rejected by the Senate, and fail to be reelected by voters.

This book is about maximizing followership skills to help achievement-motivated people realize their leadership aspirations as effectively, efficiently, and pain-free as possible. The book, however, is not just about the ascent to leadership stardom through effective followership. It is about the road to leadership through effective followership while being true to yourself—a pathway that reduces excessive self-sacrifice and compromise of one's values and character. After all, where is the unmitigated joy and self-fulfillment of leadership if you have denied your vocational passions or failed to conduct yourself in a manner that is consistent with your values? While the road to leadership is paved with compromise and sacrifice for the broader good, the road to leadership *misery* is paved with compromised morals and the denial of the inner voice that tells us who we really are.

But even more so, this book is about how to become an effective follower for those who have no aspirations to become a leader. It is for people who simply want a more harmonious, pleasant, and fulfilling work environment through pleasing the boss while being true and fair to themselves. However, before singing the praises of followership, let's not mince words. Followership has a serious downside when employees are subordinated to abusive or incompetent leaders or placed in jobs that suffocate self-expression and personal growth.

The Dark Side of Followership

Whenever you are a follower, someone has power over you, and that power in work environments has enormous significance because it affects your capacity to feed, house, and clothe your family. Consequently, followers typically do not act the way they would like to act nor do they say what they would like to say. Otherwise, a lot of us would be going to work in sweatpants or gym shorts and expressing our views with an irreverence that would a bring sparkle to the eyes of Howard Stern and the ghost of George Carlin.

The power that superiors have over their subordinates is especially problematic when bosses exercise autocratic control and a punitive approach to management. Followership can be unbearable when you are denied self-determination and self-expression or when a climate of fear casts its ominous shadow over a work environment. Even without abusive bosses, followership can be problematic if you are stuck in a boring, growth-depressed job that is beneath your level of talent and experience. As a baby boomer, the greatest waste of talent that I observed as my cohort entered the job market was the college-educated women who, stuck in male-dominant work cultures, were relegated to positions as receptionists, secretaries, and flight attendants. This is not to demean these jobs or to suggest that they are not perfect jobs for people who love them. I simply knew too many college-educated women who were unfulfilled by these jobs because they were overqualified and under-stimulated. However, the greatest tragedies of followership for any generation at any level of education are the dehumanizing assembly line jobs where individuals perform the same mind-numbing task over and over for hours and hours.

When I was a doctoral student, I had the privilege of studying public administration under the most published faculty member in the country—Robert T. Golembiewski. More than a bookworm, Dr. G., as many of us called him, was a sportsman with a backpack full of adventuresome stories. He told us about killing a wild boar with a penknife, hitting a home run in Yankee Stadium, and having the highest rating a pitcher could have in the Los Angeles Dodgers' training camp because he could throw a baseball through a one-foot diagonal hole in a net behind home plate 75 percent of the time. He also shared a fascinating ability to read without having to move his eyes because he could see two adjacent pages in a book completely in focus. More importantly, what the man said and did in the classroom was unforgettable.

Dr. G. stressed that one of the major roles of management is to move each employee into an optimal arousal zone where they experience maximum motivation and job satisfaction. Unfortunately, followers are commonly under-aroused, while leaders are often over-aroused, thus both roles often need to have their jobs redesigned (see figure 2.1 below). While this book is about learning how to be a superb follower, the emphasis is also on followers being good to themselves through, for

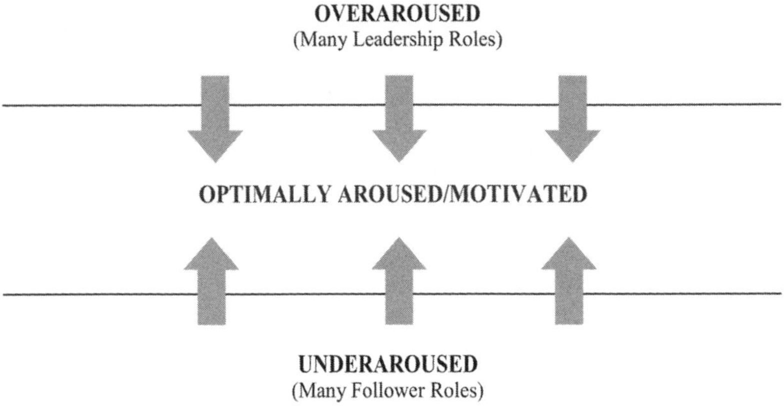

OVERAROUSED
(Many Leadership Roles)

OPTIMALLY AROUSED/MOTIVATED

UNDERAROUSED
(Many Follower Roles)

Figure 2.1   Motivation Arousal Zones

example, escaping the zone of under-arousal that Dr. G. identified as the impediment to stimulating, meaningful, and fulfilling jobs.

Followership—Good Enough for My Father

I could never understand why my father, a microbiology professor, never wanted to be a dean or department chair. He was the total package—brilliant, levelheaded, and a former college football player with an upbeat personality and a love for practical jokes. I once asked my wife to point to the person whom she thought was the most fun loving and mischievous in a 1943 picture of 52 fraternity brothers at the University of Utah. Without knowing what my deceased father looked like, she immediately pointed to him. And yes, he was the college student who liked to hit golf balls over the Beta Theta Pi house, and, yes, he once rolled a snowball on the roof of his fraternity house and dumped it on the dean, who had been a dinner guest. However, what made my father truly exceptional was that he was much more than a jock and prankster—he was incredibly smart. Needing little sleep, staying up half the night reading, and remembering everything that crossed his eyes, he was like a walking encyclopedia.

Moreover, his hand-eye coordination that enhanced his athleticism spilled over into his ability to work efficiently and effectively in laboratories where he conducted all sorts of research that was published in leading journals.

Between his brains, talent for research, strong values, and enjoyable personality, Dad was an enticing target for administrative positions. Yet he never strayed. He was a scientist—an explorer on a journey with a microscope learning about the world of organisms that cannot be seen with the naked eye but have profound effects on our lives. He was also a follower who had to comply with instructions from deans and department chairs, but like many people who make a career out of academia, he was also self-actualized in the classroom. And like so many scientists, he was so fulfilled conducting research that the status and higher pay of leadership positions could not pry him from his sanctuary—the laboratory. He was content as a follower.

The Virtues of Followership

Despite the common problems that followers face, there are advantages to being a follower that should put a smug smile on all of our faces. For one, if you are a type A canine from table 1.2—a person who does not enjoy or is not stimulated by the diverse responsibilities of leadership positions—then a follower role is likely to reduce stress and enhance job satisfaction. If you are currently placed in a narrowly defined job that allows you to focus on what you really enjoy doing, then you would be foolish to hop on the elevator to a leadership role. Doing so would not only open the door to jobs that you hate; poor performance in leadership roles can also put you on the downward escalator leading to your employer's exit door. Being fired on your employer's terms or impulsively quitting before finding another job leads to the greatest nightmare of them all—no income to support yourself or your family. Bailing out of a leadership role to land another job that is a poor fit for your skills and interests, in turn, simply trades one set of problems for another.

Unfortunately, the human ego is such a commanding motivational force that the status and recognition of leadership roles seduces people and ultimately leads to the demise of many leaders. Lawrence Peter and Raymond Hull wrote a clever, classic management book published in 1969 that attributes the frequent cause of leadership failure to what they called the "Peter Principle."[4] This principle asserts that employees rise to their level of incompetency in hierarchical organizations. Because of their competent performance at one level in an organization, Peter and Hull contend that employees are promoted to the next level in a hierarchy. This continues until they reach a level of leadership where they are no longer skillful enough to perform the responsibilities of their jobs. A crack salesperson may also be a superb manager of a sales team and even several sales teams as she or he scales the hierarchy to a mid-level leadership position based on past performance. But once such an employee rises to an executive level with responsibilities beyond sales, such as strategic planning and new product development, the job changes so dramatically that the employee no longer has the knowledge, insight, or appropriate leadership style to ensure success.

Examples of the Peter Principle are manifold. While Ulysses S. Grant is remembered as a military hero who defeated Robert E. Lee to end the Civil War, his presidency shines dimly with memories of scandals and an economic recession.[5] Lane Kiffin is one of college football's finest offensive coordinators, but a three-time failure as a head football coach. Contemporary history's best example, Adolf Hitler, was a genius as a political leader. But when he elevated himself to commander and chief of Germany's war effort in 1943, the German death toll escalated to an estimated nine million, and the worldwide death toll from World War II rose to at least 60 million.[6]

A follower's role, in contrast, eliminates the fire hydrant syndrome that all leaders experience. We all know what dogs do to fire hydrants. Well, metaphorically speaking, employees do the same thing to leaders, from the lowest level foremen to the highest-ranking CEOs. Followers escape the world of disgruntled and malcontent employees who complain about everything—their colleagues, assignments, pay, performance evaluations, lack of recognition, denial of promotions, failure to be consulted, and simply not getting their way. Followers are freed from saying no to people they genuinely care about and freed from saying no to people who will forever hold it against them. Followers are free from being a referee between battling factions or from rendering judgments in zero-sum games that create winners and losers. Moreover, they are liberated from having to fire employees and can dodge conflicts and problems that leaders are forced to address.

Ultimately, organizations have fewer reasons to terminate followers, and foes have fewer opportunities and reasons to sue followers. Although the average length of stay in a management occupation is quite high (6.9 years), a survey of approximately 5,000 executives, search consultants, and corporate human resources professionals indicates that the average tenure of a business executive is only 2.3 years.[7] While I assert, unequivocally, that abusive bosses and dehumanizing work are not to be tolerated, a follower's role in an enjoyable job with a fair and reasonable boss is typically a substantially less stressful work experience than serving in a leadership role.

The Informal Follower-Leader: A Powerbroker without the Responsibilities and Accountabilities

Have you ever been to an organization meeting totally prepared to contribute your well-reasoned and researched views, only to have your colleagues briskly dismiss your ideas or not even address them? Was the discussion minimal, and was a decision made in a fraction of the time that you anticipated? If so, the odds are that your ideas either really missed the mark or you were just snookered by the informal organization.

The informal organization is *one of the top five most significant concepts* that I teach in courses in organization behavior and organization theory. It is the organization that exists outside the formal institution's structure with its prescribed hierarchy, division of labor, rules and regulations, and official roles and responsibilities for leaders and followers. In other words, I like to describe the informal organization as *how an organization really operates* with its informal rules and norms, procedures, and hierarchy of leaders and followers. If this still does not make sense, think of the informal organization as the colleagues in your work environment who gather outside of their formal roles and work relationships. They may gather in the hallways, in the break room, behind closed doors, or in a bar at happy hour. The motivation for gathering may be purely social—because they enjoy one another—or because there is a need to discuss work-related business in a more constructive or safe environment than the formal structure.

In its negative incarnations, the informal organization can be a clique that restricts its membership and attempts to elevate itself above those excluded from the clique. If this sounds like junior high or middle school, you are right on target, but the stakes are much higher. A negative clique that is more active than passive can undermine the activities of the formal organization, impair the advancement opportunities of others, and even cause employees to be terminated. John K. Butler, professor emeritus of management at Clemson University, goes so far to assert, "The informal organization decides who gets hired, promoted, transferred, demoted, or fired. The formal organization just carries out the verdict."[8]

While I would be ethically and professionally remiss not to acknowledge the dark side of informal organizations, I am more concerned with the positive consequences of informal organizations, especially for followers. Dating as far back as 1938, Chester Barnard, president of New Jersey Bell Telephone Company, authored a pathbreaking book titled *The Functions of the Executive*. It identified the positive contributions of the informal organization as enhancing communication, organization cohesion, and the status and power of followers.[9] For example, the information shared in formal meetings or formal written communication is typically less frequent and not as complete as information that circulates through the informal organization. If it were not for the informal communication, for instance, no one would know whether employees are genuinely ready to retire or being given a golden parachute. The informal organization also allows individuals from different divisions and levels in the hierarchy to interact, to learn what is going on elsewhere and thus to feel less isolated and more connected to the broader organization. Currently, scholars also emphasize how informal networks in organizations provide advice, information, friendship, training, and the expression of feelings.[10]

As a follower, an individual may have little status in the formal organization because they are not in a leadership position. In the informal organization, however, they may have tremendous sway and true leadership power based on the merits of their ideas, knowledge, and intelligence, what French and Raven refer to as "expert power."[11] Back in 1964, Chris Argyris, a business professor at Yale, also emphasized how the informal organization affords employees the opportunity to vent true feelings—to experience an emotional catharsis—in a safer environment than a formal meeting with bosses who have the power over work assignments, performance evaluations, promotion opportunities, and salaries.[12] More importantly, Argyris, in concurrence with more contemporary research, revealed that a majority of employees rely on themselves and colleagues—the informal organization—to solve problems, especially difficult ethical dilemmas.[13] Followers interacting via their informal networks over lunch, happy hour drinks, 18 holes of golf, telephone calls after work, and conversations in the hallways at work are solving more problems than they do in any formal function at work. Moreover, being a formal follower, but an informal leader because of true merit, allows you a tremendous amount of power without all of the stressful responsibilities of being the formal leader. Recognizing your natural leadership abilities, fellow followers may burden you with information or requests for help, but unlike official bosses, you do not have to render nearly as many decisions that upset people, such as decisions about salary raises, regulation violations, disciplinary actions, promotions, and work assignments.

Taking Advantage of My Colleagues: The Real Leaders

For most of my career, my office has been wedged between the offices of a colleague with a Columbia PhD and a colleague with a Stanford PhD.

Barbara Chotiner, the Columbia PhD, went to Wellesley with Hillary Clinton as an undergraduate and wrote a dissertation under the direction of Zbigniew Brzezinski, President Jimmy Carter's national security advisor. Her desk was a collage of disarray that could only be dealt with by someone with a photographic memory or a very low anxiety for lost documents. John O'Neal, the Stanford PhD, experienced, arguably, the most demanding undergraduate program in the country at West Point, taught at Yale, and co-authored with Bruce Russett, a world-renowned political scientist in the field of international relations. His office, in turn, was Spartan and pin straight. Devoid of pictures on its walls and furnished with a variety of boxes spread here and there, for 25 years John's office always appeared as though he was still moving in.

Between these extraordinary office neighbors and my encyclopedic father, I have never interacted with colleagues assuming that I have a corner on the insight and knowledge necessary for problem-solving. Instead, I try to do what I teach in my public administration courses, which is take advantage of the brilliant colleagues surrounding me in their followership roles. If it is clear that some committee members are informal leaders, I will conscientiously work closely with them. If I meet talented followers who are unaware of their leadership potential, I will try to empower them. Ultimately, followers in informal leadership roles are often more powerful than the formal leaders.

Moreover, Neil Farmer, author of *The Invisible Organization: How Informal Networks Can Lead Organizational Change*, contends that nearly three-quarters of the leaders in any organization are not found in the formal management hierarchy.[14] Recognized as true leaders by virtue of their talent and character, the informal leaders have superb ideas and usually the power to mobilize support for or against the policies and programs emerging from the formal organization. And again, the informal follower-leader is not burdened with all of the ugly formal responsibilities of the formal leader.

Even if you have no desire or opportunities to be an informal leader, do not underestimate your power as a follower. Followers who come to meetings prepared, including having vetted their ideas with key players in the formal and informal organization, almost always get their way. Neil Farmer further contends that broader organizational change can be led by informal organization networks and that sustainable organization change necessarily always involves the integration of the formal and informal network.[15] At the macro level, we see followers exercising their political rights to determine political leaders and to kill or pass referendums and constitutional amendments. In congregational churches, not only do you see followers affecting church dogma and governance, they have played major roles in movements for the abolition of slavery, women's suffrage, temperance, and marriage equality.

Conclusion

This chapter contends that executive-level leadership positions are difficult to attain and, whether we like it or not, we are all followers. Although followership is highly problematic when one is subjected to abusive bosses or dehumanizing work, the follower role has many attractive advantages that we tend to overlook, including the tremendous power that followers enjoy as leaders in the informal organizations.

Now, the superficial answer to the question of how to be a great follower is quite simple—do everything the boss wants you to do and periodically surpass the boss's expectations. If you desire to know more specifically what leaders really wish from followers, chapter 3 presents a comprehensive review of the desirable follower characteristics found in the literature and research. But this book contends that pleasing the higher-ups is an unacceptable approach to followership without concomitantly meeting your personal need for stimulating and meaningful work that is consistent with your core values. In other words, this book intends to help you learn how to be a great follower in jobs that are interesting and fun, make a difference in the lives of others, and allow you go to bed each night at peace and without guilt and regret. For now, though, let's look at various typologies of followers and determine the type of follower that you are.

CHAPTER 3

Superlative Subordinates: The Ideal Follower

Although the leadership literature may be King Kong and the followership literature a mere mouse, enough has been written on followership to give you direction on what you should be striving for in order to become an ideal follower. In fact, this chapter presents the findings from 53 books and articles that address the desirable traits, behaviors, and skills based on a variety of criteria. I first report the desirable qualities advocated by scholars and practitioners based on their personal experience and understanding. Academics like to characterize these kinds of accounts as descriptive, qualitative, or narrative. Next, I present the desirable qualities based on data gathered from quantitative studies, also commonly referred to as empirical research.

While some academics prefer qualitative research and others gravitate toward quantitative, both camps take delight in making fun of each other. The empiricists are the number crunchers, the Billy Beanes of the world (the Oakland A's manager whom Brad Pitt portrayed in *Money Ball*). They try to quantify everything and love running all sorts of sophisticated statistical analyses that manage to escape collegial criticism because most of us have no earthly idea of what the number crunchers did and what their data printouts mean. These beloved jokers like to disparage the qualitative researcher for being mathematically challenged and, more importantly, for making all sorts of claims without any systematic evidence.

Qualitative researchers, in turn, pride themselves in the ability to explain phenomena more completely through unquantifiable observations and through attributing meaning to behavior that empiricists can only count. Understanding human phenomena through intuition, instincts, and judgment are also acceptable modes of developing knowledge for qualitative researchers. In their weaker moments, members of this camp disparage the number crunchers for painting an incomplete picture, lacking imagination, and, ultimately, not being able to explain much with their data. On a bad day, the qualitative researchers, born under an astrological water sign, and the number crunchers, born under an earth sign, together make mud.[1] But on their better days, the qualitative and quantitative researchers provide the right combination of building blocks for groundbreaking theories and social progress, so both the qualitative and quantitative research on ideal followership is presented here.

The qualitative accounts include 21 articles and books that describe effective, "good," exemplary, transcendent, synergetic, and competent followers—fairly broad, general criteria.[2] Likewise, they include six more accounts of the ideal followership qualities associated with narrower criteria such as courage, desirable reactions to unethical decisions, and ability to influence leaders.[3] Together, the 27 accounts identify 278 qualities of ideal followers.[4] More importantly, they identify many of the same qualities and therefore demonstrate a degree of consensus among scholars.

For fun, before looking at the lists of the most frequently noted ideal follower qualities, in the space that follows, write down three to five qualities that you think the ideal follower should possess.

Your Ideas on the Ideal Qualities of Followers

1. _____
2. _____
3. _____
4. _____
5. _____

Now, take a look at the leading follower qualities addressed in the literature.

The Top 10 Ideal Follower Qualities Identified in the Descriptive Literature

The numbers in parentheses are the number of times the qualities are identified by different scholars and practitioners.

- **Effective Communicator (29):** also includes being persuasive, speaking up, being open, and listening
- **Active (27):** also includes being energetic, taking initiative, participating, being proactive, and "just doing it"
- **Interpersonally Skillful (22):** also includes being diplomatic, friendly, and interactive; working well with others, building networks, and having social intelligence
- **Team Player (14):** also includes being collaborative, cooperative, interdependent, and a partner or comrade
- **Responsible (13):** also includes being accountable, doing the job, following through, receiving delegation, taking ownership, and knowing the job and how to do it
- **Developmental (11):** also includes being growth-oriented and able to build competencies and skills
- **Flexible (11):** also includes being able to adapt, cope, manage change, integrate oneself, and being a "player for all seasons"
- **Integrity (9):** also includes being honest, credible, ethical, and moral
- **Committed (8):** also includes being committed to the organization
- **Independent (8):** also includes being individualistic

If your speculative list of follower qualities coincides with the list in the literature, congratulations. You have superb common sense or impressive intuitive instincts. Moreover, if you have already developed the leading qualities on this list, pat yourself on the back, don a huge smile, close this book, and surreptitiously stick it in the mailbox of the worst follower that you know.

In contrast, if your list does not coincide with this top 10 list, I also say congratulations. You join a long list of colleagues, friends, family members, and students who have vetted this book or played this guessing game and missed the mark completely. I also say congratulations because you have the most to learn from this chapter—lesson one, what we think is common sense or intuitively correct is often not shared by others.

Let's give you one more chance to win at this guessing game by seeing if your speculative list of ideal follower qualities coincides with what 26 quantitative studies reveal to be the ideal qualities of followers.[5] This includes 12 studies investigating followership qualities associated with general criteria such as job performance and effectiveness.[6] It also includes 14 studies investigating the relationship between follower qualities and narrower positive outcomes such as organization commitment, work engagement, and self-leadership.[7] Because the practical demands associated with quantitative research limit the range of predictors that can be realistically investigated, there is a substantially smaller number of ideal follower qualities identified (87) than the 278 identified in the qualitative accounts. The leading ideal qualities therefore appear less frequently than they do in the qualitative literature. The leading ideal follower qualities found in the quantitative research are as follows:

The Top 10 Ideal Follower Qualities Identified in Quantitative Studies

Again, the numbers in parentheses are the number of times the traits, skills, or behaviors are identified by different researchers.

- **Responsible** (8): also includes being dependable, taking ownership, and doing one's job
- **Agreeable** (7): also includes being supportive, cooperative, obedient, and nonquestioning[8]
- **Compatible** (7): also includes being compatible with or having a positive effect on a leader's emotions and sense of humor in the following areas: affectation, positive affection, high agreeableness, high epistemic motivation, low agreeableness, low epistemic motivation, and self-defeating humor
- **Team Player or Cooperative** (7): also includes having strong coproduction beliefs and partnering with one's supervisor
- **Interpersonally Skillful** (6): also includes having negotiation skills, positive work relations, and respect for others
- **Competence** (6): also includes self-efficacy and having the ability to divert crises
- **Active** (5): also includes being industrious and taking initiative
- **Effective Communication** (5): also includes offering opinions and speaking up
- **Flexible** (4): also includes embracing change and aligning behavior with the leader and organization climate
- **Independence** (4): also includes being autonomous, disagreeing with an angry leader, and not being blindly obedient or insubordinate

If you look at the intersection of the qualitative and quantitative research, several ideal follower qualities drop out, and others demonstrate consistency on both lists. Follower developmental-orientation, commitment, integrity, and courage are addressed in the descriptive literature but emerge less frequently as ideal follower characteristics in the quantitative studies. However, do not count these characteristics out because the findings from the empirical studies are not all derived from open-ended questions that allow subjects to assert the importance of any ideal follower quality.

In turn, while being agreeable, compatible with leadership, and competent surface as important follower characteristics in the quantitative research, they are not as frequently addressed in the qualitative accounts of ideal followers.[9] More importantly, when I look at the combined frequency with which specific qualities are noted in both the qualitative and quantitative literature, *communicating effectively* and being *active* stand out as the two most noted qualities of ideal followers (see table 3.1). Being *interpersonally skillful* stands alone as the third most cited quality of followers. Moreover, for those who believe the empirical findings should be weighed more heavily, even tripling the value of the empirical studies fails to change these top three ideal qualities in the combined rankings. Being *responsible* and a *team player* separate out in a tie for the fourth most frequently noted qualities of ideal followers. Finally, being *adaptable* or *flexible* stands alone as the fifth most cited quality of ideal followers.

Despite what the preceding frequencies tell us, it is important that we take special note of the finding from the larger, more generalizable, and most methodologically rigorous studies on followership.[10] These studies

Table 3.1   Most Frequently Cited Ideal Follower Qualities in the Combined Qualitative and Quantitative Research

Qualities	Times Noted
Effective Communicator	34
Active	32
Interpersonally Skillful	28
Responsible	21
Team Player or Cooperative	21
Adaptable or Flexible	15
Additional Notable Qualities from the Leading Studies	
Integrity	11
Committed to the Job	10
Competence	9

Source: See endnotes 2, 3, 4, and 5.

identify all six of the leading follower qualities in table 3.1, but they also elevate the significance of the ideal follower being *competent* and *committed* to the job, as well as demonstrating *integrity*.[11]

Conclusion

I thoroughly enjoyed doing the research for this chapter because my preconceived notions about the ideal qualities of followers were inconsistent with the majority of the characteristics in table 3.1. Without knowing the content of this chapter, I would have told you to be competent, honest, responsible or dependable, and respectful of others. To possess or develop these characteristics would make you a terrific follower if you were my subordinate; however, in the absence of complete information about the environments of the organizations that you are associated with, your best generalization is to aspire to the qualities in table 3.1—to be active, an effective communicator, and interpersonally skillful. Being responsible, a team player, and flexible is also a wise idea, as is being competent, committed to your job, and a person of integrity. Yet I must also warn you that, in the presence of complete information about your organization environments, you may need to take exception to these qualities or even behave in a manner opposite to these qualities. For example, a dominant boss may necessitate your acting more passively, or a highly regulated production process that protects the health and safety of employees may dictate an inflexible approach to fulfilling your job.

Ultimately, to be a good follower, you need to be a good gambler— a follower who knows the odds and plays the odds in the absence of complete information. In other words, a good gambling follower would behave in a way that is consistent with the qualities in table 3.1. However, to be a *great* follower, you do not gamble at all. Instead, generate complete information about your organization environments and adjust your followership style to the environments, which means that you might take exception to the qualities in table 3.1.

For me to expect you to develop all nine qualities in table 3.1 or take exception to the qualities, however, is as naïve as expecting Lady Gaga to wear a little black dress for her next concert. We are creatures with inherent tendencies and learned habits that can be difficult to change; plus, some of you by nature are intractable hound dogs. Hoping that you already possess one or two of the top three ideal follower qualities, I would focus on the one that is in the greatest deficit, that is, develop either your communication skills, interpersonal skills, or capacity to be a more active follower. Because developing new skills and habits can be challenging, let's now turn to chapter 4 to see how to bring about changes in your thoughts and behaviors in order to become an ideal follower.

CHAPTER 4

Cultivating the Qualities of the Ideal Follower

In the summer of 1987, I bumped into a colleague that I will call James who was in such a good mood that I could not help but take a break to experience some vicarious pleasure in whatever was driving his elation. A fellow professor at California State University, Fullerton, James was a scholar's scholar—a fountain of knowledge with a penetrating intellect and a talent for publishing academic research despite the demands of a heavy teaching load.

As it turned out, James had just returned from a high school class reunion that was an exceptionally joyful experience for a reason that defied my imagination. James informed me that he grew up on a farm and attended grammar school in a one-room schoolhouse. When moved into a more populated junior high school, he found himself academically and socially ill-equipped to deal with a large student body that included some rougher elements than what he had been exposed to on the farm and in the one-room school. Moreover, James's mother passed away unexpectedly, leaving him without direction and the one person who brought him the greatest comfort in life. Best described as lost, James flunked every one of his classes in the ninth grade.

Through the confluence of various structures and influences, James's life slowly began to evolve in a new direction. He transferred to a different high school where he made wonderful friends and met the woman who would become his wife. Marriage shortly after high school graduation brought meaning to his life and the necessity to learn how to manage himself and his new family. In turn, James enlisted in the navy where he learned invaluable lessons about the virtues of structure and discipline in shaping his life and realizing his dreams. Tested and assessed over and over in the navy, he also became aware for the first time in his life that he was innately smart. After leaving the navy, James enrolled in a small liberal arts college in the Midwest and experienced another epiphany—he loved learning.

After two confidence-building years in a small college, James decided to go for broke by applying for admission to the University of California, Berkeley, arguably the finest public university in the country. He was accepted, attended, and excelled. With his academic rebirth complete, James went from Berkeley to Stanford University where he earned an MA and a PhD through a department of political science commonly regarded by scholars as the best in the country. James ultimately returned home to his high school reunion as an academic star. Beneath the veneer of a ninth-grade academic misfit was the soul of a class valedictorian that went unrecognized in his youth.

James's transformation did not happen overnight. But for some, change occurs with great speed and magnitude when unexpected natural disasters, divorces, health problems, wars, and financial crises turn a person's world upside down. For others, unexpected *positive* experiences also bring about fast, dramatic change.

Take my one-time agnostic friend Chris, an orthodontist whose life could best be described as charmed—good family, good looks, natural athleticism, and exceptional intelligence. Plus, he had the gift of the silver tongue, no, *platinum* tongue. Elevating his social banter to an art form, you never knew or cared whether he was telling the truth because he was so darn entertaining, likeable, and completely unpredictable in his storytelling. Moreover, when you hit the town to party with Chris, you never, I repeat, never paid a cover charge to get into any place. In fact, on a busy Friday or Saturday night when the lines for the popular hot spots were wrapped around the block, we walked straight to the front of the line and unleashed Chris's linguistic magic to gain entrance immediately for free. Yet, perplexingly, as he peaked professionally and socially with more money than he could spend, a stunning girlfriend, and all of the status that he could ever desire, Chris began to experience bouts of anxiety and depression for no apparent reason.

Willing to do whatever it took to prevail over a condition that he described as hopeless, Chris started working through a laundry list of potential means to terminate the never-ending ping-pong game between his angst and emotional funk.[1] That list included exploring religion. What happened next, he was totally unprepared for.

Checking out a Christian youth conflict seminar with 15,000 attendees packed into the Omni Coliseum in Atlanta, Chris unwittingly experienced what he came to conclude was a mild form of stigmata, wounds that reflect those that Jesus experienced during his crucifixion. A quarter-size pool of blood appeared in the palm of his right hand. Searching his body for a small cut, nosebleed, open sore, or dislodged scab, Chris came up with nothing, as did the person sitting next to him who witnessed the experience and participated in the search for an explanation. More a product and disciple of his scientific training than any theology at the time, Chris exhausted all rational explanations for the blood in his hand and concluded that it was a small miraculous sign. This positive, profound experience, in turn, brought about immediate dramatic changes in Chris's lifestyle that he concluded had been too self-centered, hedonistic, and devoid of meaning.[2]

I am sure that you have heard other religious stories that brought about immediate conversions and changes in people's lives. However, this chapter will address a process of change that is closer to James's experience than Chris's experience with a fast, dramatic change. But do not be discouraged. For those of you who are both highly intent on developing new qualities and committed to the appropriate approach, one commonly espoused timeframe for developing new habits is 21 days.[3]

Consensus on How to Bring about Personal Transformation

Although the literature on personal transformation appears extremely diverse and complex, beneath its façade, many of the approaches to change share common themes and recommendations.[4] Let's take a look at the common wisdom in the form of steps to become a more ideal follower.

Step One. "Begin with the End in Mind": A Vision and Goals

The second habit advocated by Steven Covey in his national bestseller, *The Seven Habits of Highly Effective People*, is to begin with the end in mind, or "to begin today with the image, picture, or paradigm of the end ... as your frame of reference."[5] Covey and other authorities emphasize the significance of visualizing, or imagining, the desired results with all of the positive feelings and emotions that will accompany the successful realization of your vision. Imagine how you will feel as a star follower in terms of your joy, self-confidence, contentment, and sense of security. If you are intent on mastering only one or two skills of the ideal follower, visualize yourself operating competently in that skill area with a poise and self-assurance that is palpable to others. For example, visualize working in groups knowing that you possess state-of-the-art interpersonal skills. Imagine the comfort and confidence boost, the pleasure derived from pleasing others, and the satisfaction from realizing more of what you want through the adroit exercise of your newly developed interpersonal skills. In general, develop an exhilarating dream of all of the wonderful things to come through realizing the dream. Likewise, imagine your frame of mind and emotions if you fail to realize your vision—your wounded self-worth and disappointment in falling short of your full potential.

More specifically, the experts encourage us to establish and prioritize long- and short-term goals. They also encourage us to write down our goals and post them in a prominent place (e.g., on a bulletin board, desktop, or wall) to serve as a constant reminder of the goals. While it is one thing to look at a statement of goals in language, another way to indelibly impress your goals is to put together a vision board with *pictures* of the different goals that you desire.[6]

Moreover, I am persuaded by the virtues of writing down the *reasons why* you want to achieve various short- and long-term goals. This exercise helps clarify goals, reinforce goals, and establish which goals have the highest priority. Let's assume you have a goal of developing your interpersonal skills. To reason that you want to become more interpersonally competent to be accepted by a popular clique at work would likely lead to a lower prioritization than developing interpersonal competence in order to become a more productive employee, skillful follower, or responsive agent for your clientele.

Step Two: Strategize to Realize

Personal change is facilitated and more likely to occur by developing and carrying out a thoughtful strategy for change. One rule of thumb is to develop a strategy or plan that addresses one goal at a time. Next, authorities encourage you to break goals into manageable pieces to simplify goal achievement and to allow yourself to see progress. For instance, if your goal is to become a more effective follower by developing your communications skills, you might break down this goal into two sets of three subgoals. One set of goals could be to participate in training to develop (1) verbal skills, (2) written skills, and (3) the confidence to communicate proactively, while another set of subgoals could be to identify and participate in applied opportunities to practice (4) oral skills, (5) written skills, and (6) proactive communication.

The achievement of goals is also facilitated by a strategy that establishes measurable goals and reasonable deadlines for achieving goals. However, these two elements of a strategy are not set in stone. What if your goal is to write a weekly progress report for your boss that takes no longer than a half-hour to compose? You may master the ability to craft reports in a half-hour, but that does not mean that they are adequately accurate, well-written, and complete in their content. In general, quantitative goals tend to become the object of a person's motivation to the neglect of qualitative accomplishments. Qualitative assessments of the progress that you have made toward personal goals are quintessential and an invaluable function that insightful and trusted colleagues and superiors can provide. So, swallow any shyness or pride, and ask others to share whether they have noticed any qualitative changes in your behavior.

Another common element in a plan for personal change is establishing realistic goals in order to prevent setting yourself up for failure. However, this element also has its exceptions. First, some people are capable of living with failure. In fact, people with a high need for achievement do not mind failing to meet goals as long as they are working independently, have control over the results of their efforts, and can measure the degree to which goals are achieved. In such circumstances, David McClelland, the Harvard psychology professor who popularized the study of achievement motivation, contends that people with a high need for achievement will even assume a goal where they have only a 33 to 50 percent chance of succeeding.[7] Why? Because, in the process of aspiring to difficult goals that they have control over, the person with a high need for achievement will often realize a tremendous amount of growth.

If, however, you are a person who does not have a high need for achievement or if you have no control over factors affecting your work outcomes (e.g., bad colleagues, inadequate resources and support), you may need to establish more realistic goals and deadlines. The inability to meet demanding goals can leave you downtrodden and disposed to give up far short of optimal levels of performance.

Step Three: Hang with Those Who Bring Out Your Best

In the ninth grade, my science teacher had a seating chart based on alphabetical order. With a last name beginning with B, I was placed next to a person whose last name began with A, Arthur Anderson. Like so many preacher's sons and daughters, Arthur had a wild side that made him the envy of the less venturesome wannabes in our class. Most impressively, Arthur was brilliant—arguably the smartest kid in our class—and his accomplishments backed it up. After earning the grades and test scores to matriculate at Northwestern University, Arthur hit the jackpot in being admitted to and graduating from Harvard Law.

For our purposes, Arthur's impact on me is what is relevant. As Arthur and I fast became friends, my grades went from good to great. Put simply, Arthur was a role model for academic success and an encouraging friend whose faith in my abilities gave me the confidence to become a straight A student. If you want to realize new qualities, a common admonition is to find your Arthur Anderson—an inspiring role model—and pull a monkey see, monkey do. That is, if you want to develop the ideal qualities of a follower, hang out with people who are effective communicators, proactive, and interpersonally skillful. You will learn how to behave through simply watching.

But the other change-inspiring quality of Arthur Anderson was his supportive nature, which leads to me to tell you to surround yourself with positive people, people who hold you in high regard and will support your efforts to acquire new qualities and skills. If you cannot find a role model who has accomplished what you want to accomplish, you still have promising options.

For one, you can spend more time with goal-driven people who inspire you and less time with cynics whose default tendencies are to rain on your parade for change. You can also distance yourself from people who may be civil enough not to rain on your parade but are poor aspirational examples and inadvertent bad influences on what you are trying to become. For example, if you are trying to become a more proactive follower, you can limit your time spent with passive coworkers by changing your office location, having the boss assign you to a different work team, or changing your lunch-hour routine to a time that is incompatible with the people you need to avoid. To avoid distracting people, I have been known to keep office hours in the library, request an isolated office, teach courses in different buildings, and work at home. Overall, the beauty of creating structures that facilitate becoming a more ideal follower, or whatever else you want to become, is that change is no longer a painful exercise of willpower because you have removed the temptations that feed bad habits and replaced them with structures that fuel new, desirable behaviors.

Finally, do not underestimate the capacity of good friends and family members to help you realize new goals. Ask them to remind you of your goals, to give you feedback on your progress, and, above all, to encourage your persistence in achieving your goals. If possible, find friends who understand your change objective, as well as your vulnerabilities, and give them permission to drag you from situations where temptation is about to unleash a full frontal assault on your weaknesses.[8] Ultimately, individuals with a half dozen friends who are either coaches or fans of their change are 40 percent more likely to succeed at acquiring positive new habits.[9]

Step Four: Pull a Gene Stallings—Monitor, Evaluate, Recalibrate

In 1992, I was teaching more than a dozen football players at UA and was invited to travel with the team to the Auburn game as a thank-you, as well as to serve as a visual reminder to my student-athletes of the importance of the academic side of their college experience. As part of the experience, four faculty members and I ate all of our meals at a table with the head coach, Gene Stallings. You would think that Coach Stallings would have coaches, players, athletic donors, or prize recruits sitting at his table. But, no, he surrounded himself with faculty members, and without a doubt, this got the attention of the football players I was teaching. As part of our agenda in traveling with the team, Coach Stallings invited the faculty to his suite to go over the game plan. What he proceeded to share was unexpected as we listened to this deep-voiced, slow-talking, country-rancher of a football coach describe how the coaches developed the game plan.

Coach Stallings pulled out an inch-thick computer printout that looked much like the printouts faculty generate in their academic research. Could Gene Stallings be one of us at heart? It appeared so, and that became even more convincing as he proceeded to explain the data printout and software that was generating results that dictated the game plan and the broader strategy for the football season. The printout tracked the yard line, down, play, formation, and results of every play that both Alabama and Auburn had run all season. In doing so, the data allowed Alabama to best predict and prepare for what Auburn would do in every imaginable situation during the next-day's game. Ultimately, Coach Stallings was applying a classic academic theory first popularized in 1968 by Paul Wernimont and John Campbell of the University of Minnesota called behavioral consistency theory, which asserts that the best predictor of future behavior is past behavior.[10]

All major football programs at all levels gather information to predict what their opponents will do, but the data and standards that Alabama used to monitor and evaluate the team's performance were particularly interesting. Coach Stallings was on the coaching staff of the Dallas Cowboys between 1972 and 1985 and brought to UA software that the Cowboys had used to recalibrate the team's performance on a weekly basis during their glory years under Head Coach Tom Landry.

With benchmark statistics on what it took to win the SEC Championship and National Championship, the software allowed Gene Stallings's coaching staff to identify where and to what extent the team was falling short in every performance area—the running game, passing game, passing defense, running defense, and special teams. The data were further mined to identify the performance in these dimensions on every down and yard line with different yards to go for a first down. The coaches knew how the team was performing on offense when it was third and long on their own 19-yard line or how the team was performing on defense when it was third and short on their own 8-yard line. Beyond preparing for the unique tendencies of the opponents they faced each week, practices focused on the areas where the team missed the benchmarks necessary for winning the SEC and National Championship.

So, what was the result of all of this monitoring and recalibrating of UA's football practices in 1992? UA won the National Championship by beating a highly favored University of Miami University football team, thus setting a superb example of what can be achieved through the ongoing practice of monitoring goal progress and making strategic adjustments based on the information gained from such observation.

Does that mean that you should develop benchmarks for progress that are equivalent to National Championship standards? Yes and no. If you have a high need for achievement and control over the variables affecting benchmark attainment, by all means, set lofty benchmarks. If not, take the time to establish benchmarks that are reasonable. If you are going to establish the behavior and performance of a coworker as the standard, do not pick your organization's star. Pick someone who performs at one level higher than yours. Better yet, judge your progress against your previous performance.

By using your past performance as your benchmark, you can often avoid the dejection that comes from disappointing comparisons to others. A friend of mine learned this lesson the hard way when he was teaching Introduction to Political Science as a graduate teaching assistant (GTA) at the University of Georgia. He and 21 other GTAs were ranked according to student evaluations, and he was upset that his rankings had stopped improving even though he tried to improve his teaching every quarter that he taught.

During his first year as a GTA, his student evaluation rankings made large upward leaps as he experienced a substantial learning curve as someone who had never been on the teaching end of a classroom. Given the progress made, he felt that he was well under way to becoming one of the top two or three most highly ranked GTAs. Perplexed and frustrated by the lack of progress, we took a look at his teaching evaluations over time, and guess what we found. He had improved every quarter in every area in which the student evaluations generated data. His student evaluation rankings had leveled off, not because he was failing to improve, but because he was a part of an outstanding group of GTAs who were improving at the same rate that he was.

Managing a Poor Self-Concept and Negative Evaluations

Dealing constructively with failure or a poor self-concept is a quintessential habit that needs to be added to anyone's bucket list of areas for personal development. Two keys to dealing with failure are (1) to replace destructive thoughts with rational thinking, including realistic self-assessments, and (2) to overpower negative feelings, especially pejorative self-assessments, with positive interpretations of events and positive affirmations about yourself. Just as I addressed the importance of recalibrating strategies and behavior after an evaluation of progress, I am now talking about recalibrating your mental and emotional states.

Let's assume that you have conscientiously tried to develop the interpersonal skills of the ideal follower, and your annual performance evaluation reveals that your new behavior has backfired. The boss's feedback informs you that you are too socially aggressive. To address the boss's concern, you replace immobilizing thoughts of hopelessness with a proactive effort to develop an in-depth, objective understanding of the problematic behavior and dynamics that led to that behavior. Furthermore, you also replace pessimistic assessments with constructive realizations that a failed approach is a significant lesson learned about an attractive option that, surprisingly, did not bear fruit. After all, you likely chose a course of action based on a defensible logic. To learn that the logic and its application are faulty is a significant gift of knowledge to yourself and others.

In turn, instead of regressing to youth-instilled tendencies to label yourself a chronic nerd doomed to identify with the socially inferior, you overpower negative feelings by focusing on your positive attributes. For example, you tell yourself that you are a smart, decent person, worthy of friendships across all social strata, and capable of becoming interpersonally adept. You also accurately label yourself as someone who is eager to develop the interpersonal skills of the ideal follower and realistically assess the level that you are starting at, which may, in fact, be at an intermediate or even a beginner's level of skill.

These mental approaches for coping with failure and bringing about personal change are then mastered through experimentation, practice, and repetition—that is, more practice! But the hackneyed saying that "practice makes perfect" is not enough, and I encourage you to adopt Vince Lombardi's mantra: "Perfect practice makes perfect."[11] This, in turn, requires that you refocus on your goals and stick to the implementation principles and instructions in your strategic plan that are, of course, periodically recalibrated along the way. And this isn't always easy. Although I have taught coursework in organization behavior for over 35 years, I still have to remind myself to do what I teach when I encounter people-oriented problems in my work environments. However, I can attest that, through persistent deliberate reflection and the conscious choice of different courses of action, eventually we replace old, dysfunctional habits with new, more functional habits.

Lastly, I would like to emphasize the importance of avoiding cruel self-judgments that hold us back from realizing desirable changes. Why some people are born with the genius of a Bill Gates, the entrepreneurial

GOLF—A PARAGON OF THE PITFALLS OF IMPERFECT PRACTICE

To reinforce the significance of perfect practice, go to a practice range and observe someone hitting golf balls with the ugliest golf swing on the range. Although it is obvious that this person has never had a golf lesson, he is often working longer and harder than anyone else. Yet the results are atrocious, as an improperly struck golf ball has the capacity to travel great distances in directions that would have the modular voice in your GPS swearing. This hard work, in turn, typically produces a grooved swing (a swing style that repeats itself) based on bad mechanics that result in miniscule progress toward becoming a better golfer. Because the results of a poorly hit golf ball are extreme, I have always felt that golf is more of a parody of life than an accurate metaphor for life. Regardless, the sport provides an ideal illustration of the pitfalls of imperfect practice.

talent of an Oprah Winfrey, or the athletic ability of a Michael Jordan, I cannot explain. Why the lives of wonderfully decent people can be full of tragedy and disaster is also inexplicable. But I do know that comparing your talent and life status to those with rare and richly rewarded talents is usually a dangerous habit that too often leads to feelings of inferiority and hopelessness. I concur with Professor Jeffrey Kottler, who contends that, although life is not fair and there is much that we cannot control, "The one thing that is within our power is what you think inside your own head and how you respond to the things that happen to you."[12] You are all that you have with all your literal and figurative warts and sores and scabs and scars that you did not choose. If you feel that society does not place great value on what you have to offer, at least grant yourself the self-respect that you so richly deserve as a human being.

Daniel Siegel, Harvard-trained psychiatrist and author of *Mindsight: The New Science of Personal Transformation*, contends that we should treat ourselves the way we treat friends who turn to us for help. That is, we should treat ourselves with an "open heart and a shoulder" to lean on—from a nonjudgmental, "supportive and kind" place reflecting a compassionate state of mind.[13]

Moreover, for those of you who may feel that life dealt you a handful of random number cards adding up to nothing, I will share another intense belief. If you have taken that bad hand and turned it into as little as a jack or a pair of deuces, you have lived a much more admirable and honorable life than societal elites who are dealt a handful of face cards from the moment of conception, yet accomplish little of value with their unearned privileges.

Journals and Triggers

Several authorities advocate keeping a journal of your experiences in developing new habits and skills.[14] A journal provides a superb place to record and evaluate your progress and to document adjustments to your strategic plan. The journal is also a terrific place to vent emotions, especially frustrations that, once expressed in writing, can free you up psychologically to move on to constructive behavior. I also like the idea of a journal as a place to identify (1) triggers, or crucial moments that may cause you to regress to old behaviors, and (2) substitute behaviors for bad habits once you recognize the triggers. As an example, let's say you are working to develop your interpersonal skills as a follower and find yourself shy and withdrawn in a particular situation. You might reflect on whether the shyness was triggered by something someone said, by the presence of a particular person, or by feeling particularly unattractive or distracted that day. Once you have identified the time, place, people, and physical and emotional states that cause you to regress to old ways, you are at least halfway through the process of developing new, more constructive habits.[15]

The next significant step is to identify substitute thoughts and reactions when a situation seems to be goading you into past habits. Let's assume the shyness that is blocking your interpersonal competency was triggered by a conversation topic that makes you feel stupid and insecure because you feel you have nothing to contribute to the conversation. Now that you know the trigger, you can decide what to do in similar future situations. For example, you might devise the following substitute behaviors that allow you to stay involved and actually shine in such conversations:

- *Find something that genuinely interests you in the conversation, and compliment the individual for sharing that information.* You can rarely go wrong with a sincere compliment. As I tell my students, praise and recognition won't get you to heaven, but it will get you as close to heaven on earth as possible. And the irony is that praise and recognition cost nothing and take only seconds!
- *Identify something in the conversation that you find stimulating, and ask people to elaborate on their ideas.* Most people would rather hear themselves talk instead of others, so give them center stage! This, too, enhances the self-esteem of others and leads to another saying that I share with my students—see that their egos grow, and watch their attention flow to your kind soul who sowed the seeds of their self-worth.
- *Bring shy others into the conversation.* When you solicit the input of the more silent types, you send an unspoken message: "I think that you have something of value to say." Bingo! Once again, you have enhanced feelings of self-worth in others—a wonderful interpersonal skill to develop—and opened the door to a more inclusive, stimulating conversation that is often addressed toward you because you were thoughtful enough to pay attention to those overlooked in the conversation.

In closing, you will know or learn what substitute behaviors work best for you. Use a journal to brainstorm substitute behaviors, and take comfort and delight in knowing that you have better options than old habits when temptation threatens to attack your vulnerabilities.

Accountability: The Catalyst for Accomplishment

While I love the concept of evaluating and recalibrating behavior, for some of you, recalibrating is not an issue—getting started and following through with new behavior is. To prevent fitful starts and follow-through, Patterson et al. suggest that there should be positive consequences ("bribes") for successfully developing new habits and negative consequences for failing to commit to new habits.[16] Now, if you are anything like me, the thought of applying positive and negative incentives causes recessed feelings of repulsion to surface from the bone marrow of my emotions. But if they work, why not give them a try? Moreover, if you are willing to try, why not use incentives in a stimulating competition of your choice and design?

Let's say that you are trying to improve your communication skills, and the goal is a new habit of writing a weekly memo to the boss reporting your plans for the upcoming week. For a month and a half, every time you write the memo, give yourself $20 toward something that you really want—a new dress, dinner at a five-star restaurant, tickets to a sporting event or play. Each week that you fail to write the memo, donate $20 to some legitimate cause that is antithetical to your beliefs. If the year were 2016 and you were a good Democrat, I would suggest that you force yourself to donate to Donald Trump's political campaign, and if your penchant were pachyderm politics, I would tell you to fork over $20 a week to Hillary's campaign. Interestingly, penalties have a stronger impact on defeating bad habits than equivalent rewards, and people who impose penalties on themselves defeat bad habits 50 percent more frequently than those who do not.[17] You probably know what kind of penalty that would encourage you to break with the old and stick with the new, so put the penalty in play and have some fun with a competitive game that you create!

In setting up the rules of the game, however, do not reward yourself for only reaching long-term outcomes. Persistence toward your ultimate goal will be enhanced substantially if you also reward yourself for achieving short-term goals. Moreover, rewarding yourself for taking the right steps or actions to prepare for achieving long-term goals is critical because desirable outcomes may not come immediately. For example, in your efforts to develop the communication or interpersonal skills of the ideal follower, it is essential that you reward yourself for such efforts as completing a relevant community college course, professional workshop, or in-house training program.

Another promising trick to enhance accountability for making progress toward a goal is to announce your goal to others and to post your progress toward the goal on social media sites that you and your friends frequent. Odds are that you are similar to most people who like to be true to their word, as well as demonstrate that they have the talent and fortitude to realize their goals. Like most, you probably don't relish the idea of failing at something publicly. If you care about what others think, your public pursuit of becoming a better subordinate can put a lot of pressure on yourself—but you are also stacking the deck in favor of achieving your goal.

A Plug for Higher Education—Take a Class or Two

In one of his most famous comedy routines, Don Novello plays Father Guido Sarducci, a chain-smoking Italian priest who promotes a ficti-tious university that takes five minutes to teach you everything that you would remember five years after graduating from a traditional four-year college.[18] Although Father Sarducci's assessment of learning retention hits the mark more than I would like to admit, I can say, unequivocally, that I still apply multiple principles of effective communication that I learned in an interpersonal dynamics course that I took in 1975. Before reviewing the major messages of this chapter, I therefore feel compelled to encourage you to enroll in classes that will help you develop the quali-ties of the ideal follower. Since much of this book is relevant to becoming a more active follower through working in a job you love in environ-ments that fit your followership style, I will focus my comments on the educational opportunities for developing the two other major qualities of the ideal follower—being an effective communicator and being inter-personally skillful.

Boasting over 4,200 post-secondary degree-granting institutions, our system of higher education in the United States affords us incredible opportunities for personal development.[19] Moreover, with over 80 per-cent of the U.S. population living in urban areas, most of you should have a fairly easy commute to one of these institutions.[20] And those of you in truly remote parts of the country still have superb educational opportunities through distance learning online.

If you do not have a college education, you can start working toward a college degree at any time. But that is not a necessity if you desire to develop your communication or interpersonal skills as a follower. You can always enroll as a non-degree student; plus, colleges and universities typically have what are known as continuing education programs for people who are interested in furthering their education but not desiring a degree. However, if you are willing to take a series of classes in a skill area, then you can earn a certificate that documents your accomplishment. This may help you qualify for pay raises, promotions, and more interesting work responsibilities. Continuing education programs and coursework are also appealing because they are offered in the evening, at night, and on the weekends for people who work full-time.

If you want even greater access to course work to enhance your communications and interpersonal skills, enrolling in online courses is clearly the avenue of choice. Beyond allowing you the convenience of working from your home or office, online courses are substantially less expensive than courses taken on a campus, and, most excitingly, you can take courses offered by institutions of higher education all over the world. Moreover, if your work schedule or family responsibilities are too unpredictable to allow you to take a regularly scheduled course, you can always enroll in online classes that allow you to complete the course on your own schedule because they are self-paced.

While many of you may be employed by organizations that will pay for work-related training, I am saddened that some of you may not have that good fortune. But do not worry, in recent years there has been an enormous growth of massive online open courses (MOOCs) that allow you to enroll in courses and programs *for free.* Over 4,500 MOOCs currently exist, and 74.9 percent are taught in English.[21] Not only that, many of the finest higher educational institutions in the country—UC Berkeley, Dartmouth, Harvard, MIT, Princeton, Stanford—contribute to these free course offerings.

With "communication skills" and "interpersonal skills" as key search words, table 4.1 presents the number of courses that emerge from a MOOC search of Coursera and edX, the two largest MOOC providers.[22] It also provides the results of a similar search of MOOC List, a

Table 4.1   Number of Current MOOCs Found by Searching "Communication" and "Interpersonal Skills"

Provider/ Index	Communication Skill MOOCs	Interpersonal Skill MOOCs
Coursera	391	288
edX[a]	227	183
MOOC List	1,120	63

[a]Includes self-paced courses.
Source: See endnotes 19 and 20.

ANOTHER INSPIRING STORY OF CHANGE

Steve was a classmate who had it all—star athleticism, good looks, and a quick wit that rivaled the brutality of the hits he routinely delivered on the football field at Athens High School in the late 1960s. In fact, the first day I walked onto the football team at Athens High, Steve hit me so hard in a contact drill that he knocked the helmet off my head (a first!) and left welts on my neck that made it appear as though I was trying to set a Guinness World Record for number of hickies on a teenage neck. He never said a thing about his violent masterpiece for which I was his canvas, but his mind was easy to read: "Welcome to Athens High, you hick from Kentucky. If you're gonna make this football team, you're gonna have to come through me." I sensed that Steve did not like me, but I fast learned not to take him personally because, frankly, he did not seem to like anyone. I can still visualize Steve—Athens High's Cool Hand Luke—running laps for punishment because he couldn't resist defying even the head football coach.

Fast-forward to our 20-year high school reunion. After an hour of cocktails, the emcee called everyone to their dinner tables. What happened next had me choking on my beer. The emcee called on Steve to share a blessing over the food. What? Was this a joke, an accident, or just a mindless invitation for someone to spit back some meaningless, cliché blessing? Or had Steve found God? We were all fascinated to learn that Steve had attended a Calvinist seminary and was now running a Christian counseling center that he had started in Athens. To this date, no one in our graduating class of roughly 500 students has made a bigger difference in the lives of others than Steve. The one-time instrument of physical pain on the practice field and mental pain off the field is now the instrument of the Lord healing wounded spirits and filling empty souls. For the purposes of this book, he is the poster child for change and an inspiring example of how we all can become something different, something special.

search engine that indexes MOOCs from all of the known providers.[23] Although the number of MOOCs relevant to your *specific* interests will be smaller than those in table 4.1, there will still be an abundance of courses that will help you develop the skills that you desire.

Recap: Secrets to Successful Change

This chapter is quite dense with instructions, so let me simplify and summarize the eight major secrets for bringing about change that will help you become an ideal follower.

1. Begin with an enticing vision of the follower quality or skill that you want to develop, and imagine all of the pleasurable feelings that will accompany acquiring the quality or skill.
2. Develop a strategy that breaks down your vision into manageable goals or parts, thus allowing you to enjoy short-term and intermediate progress.
3. Surround yourself with role models and friends whom you can count on to support your effort to become an ideal follower.
4. Monitor your progress, and recalibrate your behavior when you don't meet benchmarks.
5. When efforts fall short or fail, replace harsh criticism of yourself with positive self-affirmations and rational thoughts about how next to proceed.
6. Keep a journal in which you identify the triggers that cause you to regress to undesirable habits.
7. Develop, experiment with, and practice, practice, practice substitute behaviors to implement when crucial moments trigger the temptation to regress to old habits.
8. Implement entertaining games with personally tailored rewards and penalties for achieving and failing to achieve desirable qualities and skills.

CHAPTER 5

What Kind of Follower Are You? Finding Your Followership Style

Numerous scholars have developed typologies, or categories, of followers with the intent of helping leaders better understand how to manage subordinates with different natures and needs. However, we want to identify your style of following to help discern the type of leaders, organizational cultures, and organizational climates that you are most compatible with. So, let's take a look at the different types of followers in table 5.1.[1] What do you see? My first reaction is, "What in the world did Kurt Madden experience to have him write about the creepy follower?" Likewise, Steger, Manners, or Zimmerer must have had a bad experience or two to cause them to write about the kamikaze follower.

Seriously, at the most general level, I see a lot of different follower types—in fact, 90. This leads to major theoretical and practical problems. When typologies or theories become too complex or cluttered with variables, we fail to achieve parsimony, or to capture the essence of something with the most simple typology or explanation. Violating the principle of parsimony is like making a batch of cookies needing one cup full of sugar but instead using four different ingredients that, when combined, contain the needed amount of sugar. Because you use four ingredients instead of one, baking cookies becomes costly, wasteful, and time consuming; plus, the recipe results in cookies with a compromised taste. So let me attempt to reduce the number of typologies to something more workable. You may not agree completely with how I reduce the types, but bear with me to prevent the minutia from detracting from the value of the broader points that I am trying to make.

Table 5.1 Types of Followers and Typology Foundations

Blackshear (2004)—Based on Five Stages of Dynamic and Changing Followership	**Howell and Mendez (2008)— Based on Roles**
• Committed	• Interactive
• Effective	• Independent
• Employee	• Independent Cross Purposes
• Engaged	• Shifting
• Exemplary	**Jaussi et al. (2008)—Types of Creative and Innovative Followers**
Burns (1978)	
• Active	• Creative Static
• Close	• Creative Supporter
• Participatory	• Creative Skeptic
• Passive	• Creative Catalyst
Carsten, Uhl-Bien, West, Patera, and McGregor (2010)—Based on Follower Roles as Defined by Followers	**Kellerman (2008)**
• Active	• Activists
• Passive	• Bystanders
• Proactive	• Diehards
	• Isolates
Chaleff (2009)—Based on Support for the Leader and Willingness to Challenge the Leader	• Participants
	Kelley (1992, 2008, 2009)— Based on Critical Thinking and Participation
• Implementer	• Alienated
• Individualistic	• Conformist
• Partners	• Exemplary/Star/ Effective
• Resource	• Passive/Sheep
Collinson (2006)—"Identities" of Followers	• Pragmatists
• Conformity	• Yes-People
o Deferential Follower	**Kelley (1992, 2008)— Based on Paths of Followership**
o Upwardly Mobile Knowledge Worker	• Apprentice
• Dramaturgical	• Comrade
• Resistant	• Disciple
Collinson (2009)— Post-Structuralist Identities/Selves	• Dreamer
	• Lifeway
• Conformist	• Loyalist
• Resistant	• Mentee

Latour and Rast (2004)—A Kelley Adaptation Based on Critical Thinking and Participation

- Alienated
- Effective
- Sheep
- Yes-People

Lipman-Blumen (2005)—Based on Willingness to Obey Toxic Leaders

- Benign
- Leader's Entourage
- Malevolent

Madden (2011)

- Active
- Brainiac
- Complainer
- Creepy
- Default
- Fans
- I-Should-Be-the-Boss
- I-Want-to-Be-the-Boss
- Meek
- Mindlessly Loyal
- No Clue
- Puppy Dog
- Resistant
- Righteous
- Synergetic

Rosenbach, Pittman, and Potter (2012)—Based on Relationship Initiative and Performance Initiative

- Contributor
- Partner
- Politician
- Subordinate
- Disguised

Shamir (2004)—Based on the Motivations of Followers

- Calculated

- Identity-Based
- Meaning-Based
- Position-Based
- Safety-Based

Shamir (2007)—Roles in Relation to Leaders

- Recipients of Leader Influence
- Moderators of Leader Impact
- Substitutes for Leadership
- Constructors of Leadership

Steger, Manners, and Zimmerer (1982)—Based on Desire for Self-Enhancement and Desire for Self-Protection

- Achiever
- Apathetic
- Artist
- Bureaucrat
- Deviant
- Donkey
- Game Player
- Kamikaze
- Super Follower

Sy (2010) and Epitropaki, Sy, Martin, Tram-Quon, and Topakas (2013)

- Industrious
- Enthusiastic
- Good Citizen
- Conforming
- Insubordinate
- Incompetent

Zaleznik (1965)

- Compulsive
- Impulsive
- Masochistic
- Withdrawn

Source: See endnote 1.

Table 5.2 The Followership Types Constituting the Five General Types/ Continuums of Followers

General Type/ Continuum	Synonym Follower Types	Antonym Follower Types
Active-Passive	active/activist (4), proactive, achiever, engaged, participant/ participatory (3), contributor, exemplary (2), diehards, synergetic, super follower, effective (2), star, dreamer, kamikaze, apprentice, artist, lifeway, comrade, conformist, bureaucrat, malevolent	passive (3), apathetic, bystander, meek, donkey, resistant (2), sheep, alienated (2), compulsive, isolate, game player, deviant, default, resource
Conformist-Individualist	conformist (2), yes-people, deferential, subordinate, implementer, bureaucrat, employee, super follower, mindlessly loyal, loyalist, apprentice, disciple, puppy-dog, benign, leader's entourage, position-based	individualist, deviant, isolate, resistant (2), impulsive, exemplary (2), alienated (2), partner, effective, kamikaze, brainiac, independent
Committed-Alienated	committed, diehard, fan, mindlessly loyal, loyalist, puppy dog, synergetic, apprentice, comrade, disciple, dreamer, lifeway, close, creepy (e.g., stalker), interactive, leader's entourage	alienated (2), withdrawn, complainer, dreamer (when disillusioned), default, resource, independent, cross-purposes
Pragmatist-Dreamer/ Impractical	pragmatic, calculated, safety-based, apprentice, benign, lifeway	impulsive, artist, kamikaze
Self-Oriented-Altruistic	upwardly-mobile knowledge worker, game player, dramaturgical, safety-based, I-should-be-the boss, I-want-to-be-the-boss, calculated, identity-based, malevolent	lifeway (otherwise the closest might be exemplary), effective, diehards, super follower, synergetic, mindlessly loyal

Note: The numbers in parentheses are the times that different scholars used the exact language to identify a specific follower type.

Since many of the 90 followership types are fairly synonymous, I have grouped them based on their definitions (see table 5.2).[2] This process derived 5 followership dichotomies based on 83 of the 90 types. The five basic followership dichotomies are as follows:

1. Active versus Passive
2. Conforming versus Individualistic
3. Committed versus Alienated
4. Pragmatic versus Idealistic
5. Self-Oriented versus Altruistic (Other-Oriented)

To reveal your followership style, answer the questions in the Followership Typology Survey (see table 5.3). Most readers will be able to complete the survey in three minutes. If some of the questions seem repetitive, do not be concerned. That is actually good because it strongly suggests that the questions are, in fact, measuring the same thing—the followership types that we want to measure. Moreover, be sure to be brutally honest in answering the questions because otherwise the results are meaningless.

When you are finished with the survey, utilize table 5.4 to score the survey and determine your followership type. Understanding a nuance in the scoring, however, is essential. The survey purposefully includes negative statements, or statements opposite to the concept being measured. Including such statements helps prevent a response bias caused by survey respondents circling all the same answers—for example, straight sixes—to get through the survey fast and mindlessly. The opposite statements force respondents to take more time to read the statements and think about their responses. All of this is to say that your answers to the negative statements need to be reversed through subtracting them from eight. For instance, when subtracted from eight, a seven response becomes a one response and a one response becomes a seven. Ultimately, responses to questions that reflect alienation are reversed to become measures of commitment, while questions about individualism are reversed to reflect conformity.

Let me walk you through the process to determine how committed a follower you are. For questions 1, 5, and 9, enter your responses in the far right column of table 5.4. For questions 3, 7, and 11—the questions that reflect alienation, the opposite of committed—put your responses in the first blank space next to the minus sign. Now, subtract your response from eight and put that number in the far right column. Finally, add your six responses to the questions on commitment for your final score. Your score for each follower type can range from a low of 7 to a high of 42. Scores above 21 indicate that you are a committed, conforming, active, pragmatic, and self-oriented follower. Scores below 21 indicate that you

Table 5.3   Followership Typology Survey

Instructions: Circle the number that best describes your agreement with each statement.

	Strongly Disagree	Disagree	Neutral		Agree	Strongly Agree
A. Think about your level of commitment and conformity to your employer's needs.						
1. Because I am committed to our leadership, I work hard to achieve the goals of my job.	1	2	3	4	5	6	7
2. I'm more inclined to fit in than to be different from others at work.	1	2	3	4	5	6	7
3. I am so disillusioned that I no longer feel like a part of my employer.	1	2	3	4	5	6	7
4. I behave on the basis of my own standards, not the organization's.	1	2	3	4	5	6	7
5. My devotion compels me to develop skills to become a greater asset to my employer.	1	2	3	4	5	6	7
6. Although I may disagree with leaders, I will comply with their expectations.	1	2	3	4	5	6	7
7. I do not care about the same things that my employer cares about.	1	2	3	4	5	6	7
8. The way that I conduct myself at work is different from my colleagues.	1	2	3	4	5	6	7
9. My dedication drives me to do more than my fair share of the work.	1	2	3	4	5	6	7

10. I conform to what my leader establishes as acceptable behavior.	1	2	3	4	5	6	7
11. If a better job came along, I would be out of here in a heartbeat.	1	2	3	4	5	6	7
12. I question the decisions of leaders rather than follow blindly.	1	2	3	4	5	6	7

B. Now reflect on your motivation level and whether you're motivated by practical or ideal goals.

13. I put in long hours at work because I like to stay busy.	1	2	3	4	5	6	7
14. I prefer to pursue reasonable goals versus ideals.	1	2	3	4	5	6	7
15. I am a person who watches more than participates in my organization.	1	2	3	4	5	6	7
16. I'd rather shoot for the moon than a doable, compromised end.	1	2	3	4	5	6	7
17. When the demands from work slow, I still maintain a high level of activity.	1	2	3	4	5	6	7
18. I make decisions that I know will work.	1	2	3	4	5	6	7
19. I'd rather have a laid-back job than a job that requires a lot of effort.	1	2	3	4	5	6	7

(continued)

57

Table 5.3 (continued)

	Strongly Disagree	Disagree		Neutral		Agree	Strongly Agree
20. I have intriguing ideas— they're just not feasible.	1	2	3	4	5	6	7
21. I'd rather take the initiative to solve a problem than wait for someone else to act.	1	2	3	4	5	6	7
22. I don't waste my time on projects that are unlikely to succeed.	1	2	3	4	5	6	7
23. When I complete a project, I prefer a break from work rather than a new project.	1	2	3	4	5	6	7
24. I'd rather pursue dreams than what's practical.	1	2	3	4	5	6	7
C. Finally, are you more altruistic or self-promoting?							
25. I prefer a low-paying job helping others over a high-paying job that doesn't help others.	1	2	3	4	5	6	7
26. Everything I do at work is to further my career.	1	2	3	4	5	6	7
27. By choice, I spend most of my time trying to attend to the needs of others.	1	2	3	4	5	6	7
28. If people don't have something to offer me, then I don't have time for them.	1	2	3	4	5	6	7
29. I don't want recognition; I want to serve others.	1	2	3	4	5	6	7
30. I'll do whatever it takes to get ahead.	1	2	3	4	5	6	7

Table 5.4 Table for Scoring the Typology Survey

Alienated vs. Committed		Response
Question 1		= _____
Question 5		= _____
Question 9		= _____
Question 3 = 8 – (minus)	_____	= _____
Question 7 = 8 –	_____	= _____
Question 11 = 8 –	_____	= _____
Under 21 = alienated Over 21 = committed	Total	= _____

Conforming vs. Individualistic		Response
Question 2		= _____
Question 6		= _____
Question 10		= _____
Question 4 = 8 –	_____	= _____
Question 8 = 8 –	_____	= _____
Question 12 = 8 –	_____	= _____
Under 21 = individualistic Over 21 = conforming	Total	= _____

Passive vs. Active		Response
Question 13		= _____
Question 17		= _____
Question 21		= _____
Question 23 = 8 –	_____	= _____
Question 15 = 8 –	_____	= _____
Question 19 = 8 –	_____	= _____
Under 21 = passive Over 21 = active	Total	= _____

Idealistic vs. Pragmatist		Response
Question 14		= _____
Question 18		= _____

(continued)

Table 5.4 (*continued*)

Question 22	=	_____
Question 16 = 8 – _____	=	_____
Question 20 = 8 – _____	=	_____
Question 24 = 8 – _____	=	_____
Under 21 = idealistic		
Over 21 = pragmatic	Total =	_____

Altruistic vs. Self-Oriented	**Response**	
Question 26	=	_____
Question 28	=	_____
Question 30	=	_____
Question 25 = 8 – _____	=	_____
Question 27 = 8 – _____	=	_____
Question 29 = 8 – _____	=	_____
Under 21 = altruistic		
Over 21 = self-oriented	Total =	_____

Scoring Instructions. For the first three questions (e.g., 1, 5 and 9) associated with each dichotomy, enter your response in the far right-hand column. For the next three questions (e.g., 3, 7, and 11), put your responses in the first blank space next to the minus sign. Next, subtract your response from eight and put that number in the far right hand column. For your final score on each follower dichotomy, add your six responses to the questions.

are a more alienated, individualistic, passive, idealistic, and altruistic follower.

Conclusion

Given that there are 32 possible combinations of the 5 dyadic followership styles, I cannot think of anything more tedious than to write and read about all 32 combinations. However, in the following chapter, we will first identify the most common types of leadership styles, organizational cultures, and organizational climates that exist and then establish the various followership styles that are compatible with each. As indicated in chapter 1, it is not enough to tell you how to be the perfect follower. The goal is to help you become a happy and satisfied follower, which is contingent on being paired with the right leader, organizational culture, and organizational climate.

CHAPTER 6

Follower Havens and Hades: Winning through Finding the Right Fit for Your Followership Style

Follower Incompatibilities and Compatibilities—the Band Experience

During the 2004–2005 academic year, an unlikely convergence of phenomena brought about a new experience in my life that is particularly relevant to my understanding of followership. That fall, my wife and I gathered in Athens, Georgia, with family members to attend a University of Georgia (UGA) football game. At the time, my brother-in-law was the athletics director, and we were seated in his skybox with family, friends, and donors to UGA Athletics.

Trying to be a good family host, I sat down next to a young man whose appearance screamed to me that he was out of place. With tailored blue jeans, a slick auburn brown leather jacket, and highlighted hair spiked a tad in the front, he seemed far too *GQ* and metrosexual for the good ole Southern boys and bubbas dressed in khakis and Polo shirts or T-shirts, jeans, and hats advertising farm equipment. As it turned out, the young man had attended UGA and was currently living in Los Angeles. Given that I too had attended UGA and lived in LA, we bonded over our commonality for around 20 minutes before I moved on to speak to some other guests.

As I got up to leave, however, I asked him a parting question: "What do you do for a living in LA?" He modestly replied that he hosts a radio show and a television show. I then asked him the name of the television show, and he calmly replied, *American Idol*. Not being a viewer and not knowing that it was the most highly viewed show on television, I walked off after uttering to Ryan Seacrest, a total stranger to me, one of the more cavalier compliments in my life: "Huh?" pause, "I think my wife watches that show." Crowned Dumbbell-of-the-Year by my family, I proceeded to start watching *American Idol* in order to become a little more hip to the contemporary television and music scene.

Shortly thereafter, I began a sabbatical leave where I worked at home on a research project freed from all teaching, advising, and committee responsibilities. Without much variation in my work routine and without interaction with students and faculty, I became bored and in need of some stress relief. Being a new fan of *American Idol*, I felt more compelled than normal to let off some steam by wailing songs from the balcony overlooking my great room. From the balcony, my voice took on a pleasant resonance, and the amplification was so loud that I deluded myself into feeling like a rock star as I belted such oldies as "Jumpin' Jack Flash," "Vehicle," and "Try a Little Tenderness."

Spring semester of 2005, Graham Hixson, president of a dinner-debating society at UA comprised of students, faculty, and staff, invited its members to participate in an end-of-the-year talent show that the society put on for itself and senior citizens in a local retirement home. With my newfound joy of balcony belting, I consented to participate.

The event arrived, the crowd gathered, and I nervously sang "Unforgettable" by Nat King Cole to around 50 senior citizens and 40 students. The reaction of the senior citizens to everyone's performances was more reserved than I anticipated as I proceeded to become excessively paranoid thinking about the second song that I was going to sing later in the program. To humor the students, I intended to sing a totally over-the-top version of "Vehicle" by the Ides of March where, among other antics, I held a tenor high C note until I was about to pass out.

All I can say is thank God for Graham. Before I returned to perform, he took the stage dressed in drag to do a stand-up comedy routine wherein he repeatedly cradled and lifted his artificial breasts that kept drifting to the level of his belly button. Realizing that I would no longer be the sole "what-the-hell-was-that?" entertainment for the evening, I went ahead and sang my outrageous song.

In a subsequent newsletter that was sent to all current and former members of the dinner-debating society, Graham wrote a column that reviewed everyone's performance at the talent show. My performance was described with a word my parents had used when I was in serious trouble. My vocal performance was described as "astounding." I was confused.

After several dips into the spiked eggnog at a faculty holiday party the following fall semester, I broke down and told Alan, a professor of chemical engineering and a guitarist, about the confusing review of my vocal performance. Alan had no idea what "astounding" meant, but after several beers and a dip or two into the eggnog, his curiosity got the best of him. He invited his colleague, Kevin, a bass-playing aerospace engineer, and me over to his house to hear what was going on. The vocals apparently were not astoundingly bad, and our trio not only clicked musically, it clicked enough to invite Steve, a drum-playing political science professor, and Mike, a keyboardist and hospital administrator, to join us the following week. We were forming a band.

Participating in sports instead of music growing up, I had no ability to play an instrument, read music, or conceive of being a lead singer in a band. After all, every time I tried to sing along with Paul McCartney, Adam Levine, or Smokey Robinson, I could not hit the high notes. In my ignorance, I had no idea that most men are baritones and can only sing the songs of first tenors if the key is lowered. Needless to say, I was necessarily a colossal follower in this newly formed band. More specifically, I was a committed, active follower who was moderately pragmatic and somewhere between a conformist and individualistic follower.

I use a band as an organizational example relevant to followership for two reasons: bands have to make boatloads of decisions early on, and the quality of the musical product delivered is highly interdependent. Band members have to decide what music to play, how to play it, when to practice, where to play, how often to practice and play, how much to charge for gigs, what to wear to gigs, et cetera. Ultimately, the interpersonal dynamics and organization culture of a band evolve rapidly and are readily identifiable. In fact, because of the high level of intimacy necessary in producing music, being in a band has been aptly described as a polygamous marriage to your bandmates without the fringe benefits.

So, how did my followership style match up with the organization culture and leadership style in the band? The general culture of the band could be described as democratic, especially with respect to deciding on what music to play. Because all of us worked full time, the business side of the band—marketing the band and booking gigs—was fairly laissez-faire, which worked especially well with my activist and committed nature. No one seemed to mind that I took initiative to find gigs, put together a band brochure, and develop some calling cards.

By contrast, the leadership dimension of the band developed informally and was semi-authoritative with respect to when we practiced and how we arranged the music. Our keyboardist, Mike, was a superb musician who had been in an extremely popular band that had opened for such stars as B. B. King, Bill Withers, and The Grass Roots. In fact, his band had been so popular that a young, up-and-coming band from Tuskegee, Alabama, by the name of The Commodores, opened for his band one night. Having "been there, done that," Mike, understandably, wanted to be in a recreational band rather than a band that practiced and performed regularly. Plus, because he was such a fine musician, he naturally took the lead in instructing the band members on how to play oldies ranging from "My Girl" to "Born to be Wild."

What my good friend Mike wanted from the band and what I wanted were understandably different. When we met, he had been playing in bands for around 40 years. My experience totaled two weeks. Musically, he was equivalent to a doctoral student. I was in the second grade. As you can imagine, at times, my followership style of high commitment and activism was incompatible with Mike's semi-authoritative leadership style and commitment to the band. Caught between a conformist and individualist followership style, my second-grade level of questioning and ideas was, undoubtedly, difficult to tolerate.

After four years, Mike's musical commitments and interests drifted from the type of cover band that we had become, so he moved on. He was replaced by a young man named Jonathan who was too new to the band to possess the social capital necessary for calling the shots on how we played the music and when we practiced and performed. My followership incompatibilities with Mike, our departed leader, went away, and my stress level subsided substantially.

Now eight and one-half years into the band's existence, including three years of vocal lessons and a dozen singing competitions, my followership style has evolved. I have become more passive, conforming, and moderate in commitment. Meanwhile, Jonathan's job necessitated a move to Nashville, and we needed a keyboardist. Guess who we turned to, and guess who consented to play with us. Mike. What's the relationship like? It's great. Although I suspect I am still no more advanced than a middle-school kid with respect to my knowledge and understanding of music, my followership style is now much more compatible with Mike's leadership style, and the band experience couldn't be any better.

So, are you compatible or incompatible with the dynamics of the organizations in which you have membership? Having determined your followership style in chapter 3, let's now take a look at what leadership styles, organizational cultures, and organizational climates are most likely to make you happy or unhappy. First, however, I want to establish the most commonly researched leadership styles and organizational cultures and climates.

Leadership Styles, Organizational Cultures, and Organizational Climates

The litany of different types of leadership styles is longer than the types of followership styles identified in chapter 5. However, there are seven leadership styles that defy trendiness and persist in academic literature over time. These leadership styles are:

1. task-oriented
2. people-oriented
3. democratic
4. autocratic
5. laissez-faire
6. charismatic
7. transformational

Table 6.1, in turn, presents the 10 most commonly studied organizational cultures and 10 most commonly studied organizational climates in the academic literature.[1] Academic research and literature provide a variety of definitions to these concepts and go to extreme lengths to distinguish between the two.[2] Organizational culture is commonly defined as a set of shared assumptions about the world and the values and beliefs that establish expectations and guide behavior in organizations.[3] An organizational climate, in turn, is the employees' perceptions of what an "organization is about," or their "summary perceptions of an organization's work environment," including policies, practices, and procedures.[4] I like to think of the organization climate as the surface *personality* of an organization, while organization culture is analogous to the *character* of a person, or a more in-depth statement of an organization's core values and beliefs.[5]

Let's identify where there is some overlap between leadership styles, cultures, and climates to simplify our initial investigation of follower compatibilities (see figure 6.1). Figure 6.1 reveals that high-performance, task-focused orientations and caring, people-focused orientations are the two most commonly studied leadership styles, organizational cultures, and organizational climates. Moreover, authoritative dominance and democratic participation are both popular leadership styles and organization cultures to investigate. Finally, academic research and literature abounds with studies on ethical, innovative, and learning organizational

Table 6.1   Common Organizational Cultures and Climates

Ten Most Common Organizational Cultures	Ten Most Common Organizational Climates
1. Innovative, entrepreneurial, creative	1. Ethical
2. Military in nature	2. People- or human relations-oriented; warm, caring, and considerate; "getting along"; intimacy; social; affiliative
3. Learning, training and developmental	3. Innovative and creative
4. Ethical	4. High performance, productive, task- and achievement-oriented, "work hard," driven by efficiency or effectiveness
5. Bureaucratic, structure- and procedure-oriented, driven by control or rules	5. Service or customer-oriented
6. Collaborative, cooperative, team-oriented	6. Just or fair
7. High performance; task-, results-, or mission-oriented; effective; driven by accomplishment, achievement, success, or mission	7. Learning, training and developmental
8. People-oriented, including respectful of people	8. Safety-driven
9. Authoritative, dominant	9. Psychological
10. Participative	10. Autonomous, including job autonomy

Source: See endnote 1.

cultures and climates. Given the significance of these different leadership styles, cultures, and climates, let's now see how they fit with your followership styles. If you prefer tables to text, peruse tables 6.2 and 6.3 to identify the compatibilities and incompatibilities with different followership styles. Moreover, feel free to read only the sections in the text and tables that address the compatibilities and incompatibilities with your specific followership style.

Figure 6.1   Overlapping Organizational Leadership Styles, Cultures, and Climates

Active Follower Compatibilities

If you are an active follower who is properly trained and a person of good character, you are truly one of the crown jewels of followership. Because they keep you busy, high performance, task-oriented organizations are an obvious fit for you. Democratic leaders and participatory organizations will also typically provide you with more opportunities for activity than more autocratically run organizations. And, as a rule, entrepreneurial and innovative cultures and climates, as well as transformational leaders, will afford you a more active work environment than organizations that are content to maintain the status quo with respect to methods of operation and goods and services provided. However, I contend that the most appealing organization climate for active followers is the autonomy climate found in table 6.1 that is typically associated with

Table 6.2 Followership Style Compatibilities with Different Leadership Styles, Organizational Cultures, and Organizational Climates

Active Follower
- Task-Oriented leaders, cultures, and climates
- Democratic/participative leaders and cultures
- Transformational leaders
- Learning cultures and climates
- Innovative cultures and climates
- Autonomy climates

Committed Follower
- Task-Oriented leaders, cultures, and climates
- Learning/development cultures and climates
- Customer-Oriented climates
- All leadership styles, cultures, and climates when they do not betray the basis for the commitment

Conforming Follower
- Military culture
- Bureaucratic cultures
- Team cultures
- People-Oriented leaders, cultures, and climates
- Authoritative/dominant cultures
- Charismatic leaders

Practical Follower
- Democratic leaders and cultures
- Safety climates
- Utilitarian and ethical cultures and climates

Self-Oriented Follower
- People-Oriented leaders, cultures, and climates
- Laissez-faire leaders
- Developmental cultures and climates
- Autonomy climates

- Entrepreneurial cultures
- All leadership styles, cultures, and climates when they are self-serving

Immutably Passive Followers
- Autocratic and authoritative leaders and cultures
- Bureaucratic leaders and cultures
- Team cultures
- Autonomous cultures

Symptomatically Passive Follower
- Autonomy climates
- Learning and development cultures and climates
- Entrepreneurial, innovative, and creative cultures and climates
- Customer-Oriented climates
- Caring, people-oriented leaders, cultures, and climates (for burnout)

Alienated Follower
- Laissez-faire leaders
- Autonomous climates
- Ethical cultures and climates
- Justice/fairness climate
- People-Oriented leaders, cultures, and climates
- Transformational leaders

Individual Follower
- Laissez-faire leaders
- Autonomy climates
- Innovative and creative cultures and climates

Dreamer/Impractical Follower
- Innovative and creative cultures and climates

- Learning cultures and climates
- Laissez-faire leaders
- Transformational leaders
- Idealistic and ethical cultures and climates

Altruistic/Other-Oriented
- Customer-Oriented climates
- Laissez-faire leaders
- Autonomous climates
- Ethical cultures and climates

Table 6.3 Followership Style Incompatibilities with Different Leadership Styles, Organizational Cultures, and Organizational Climates

Active Follower
- Autocratic leaders
- Authoritative/dominant cultures
- Bureaucratic cultures
- Safety climates
- Any leadership styles, cultures, and climates that do not keep you busy

Committed Follower
- Bureaucratic cultures
- Innovation cultures and climates (when threatening commitment to the status quo)
- Any leadership style, culture, or climate when it violates the basis for your commitment

Conforming Follower
- Innovative/creative cultures and climates
- Transformational leaders
- Laissez-faire leaders

Practical Follower
- Innovative (unless practical) climates and cultures
- Autocratic leaders and cultures (unless the autocratic is practical)
- Deontological ethical cultures and climates

Self-Oriented Follower
- Autocratic leaders
- Dominant, authoritative cultures
- Democratic leaders and cultures
- Idealistic and ethical cultures and climates

- All leadership styles, cultures, and climates when working against your self-interest

Immutably Passive Follower
- High performance and task-oriented leaders, cultures, and climates
- Transformational leaders
- Participative cultures
- Learning/development culture and climates
- Entrepreneurial cultures and climates

Symptomatically Passive Followers
- Autocratic leaders
- Authoritative/dominant cultures
- Bureaucratic cultures

Alienated
- Autocratic leaders
- Authoritative/dominant cultures
- Bureaucratic cultures

Individual Follower
- Autocratic leaders
- Authoritative/dominant cultures
- Bureaucratic cultures

Dreamer/Impractical
- Authoritative/dominant cultures
- Bureaucratic cultures
- Safety climates

Altruistic/Other-Oriented
- Any leadership styles, cultures, and climates when it works against a follower's altruism

more laissez-faire leadership. With autonomous control over your job, you have the power and opportunity to be as active as you desire. One of the most important messages that I half-jokingly share with students when lecturing on the art of leadership is to give employees the freedom to do their jobs any way that they would like. (Just don't get thrown in jail or get the company sued!)

Your active nature, in turn, has the greatest potential to be thwarted by dominant, autocratic leaders, bureaucratic work environments, and, sometimes, safety-oriented climates. Although dominant, autocratic leaders may give you demanding job assignments that keep you active, they also impede activity by hoarding power and preventing others from participating in decision-making. Inactivity is also more likely to occur with autocratic leaders and bureaucratic organizations because subordinates often wait idly on decisions from above because they are not empowered to take initiative. The necessity of issues having to travel up and down the bureaucratic hierarchy for resolution and action will also periodically inhibit your penchant for activity, as will the rule-laden nature of both bureaucracy- and safety-oriented environments.

Committed Followers—1992 National Championship Team

As indicated in chapter 4, I traveled with the 1992 National Championship football team when they played their biggest rival, Auburn. The jocks that I was teaching that semester were always amusing. I was particularly humored when a massive interior lineman would duck his head while sneaking out of class early as though reducing his height from six feet, five inches to six feet, three inches would somehow make him invisible.

The minute I boarded the team bus for Birmingham, Alabama, where the game was to be played at Legion Field the next day, I was frequently surprised. To start, the athletes and the professors were each greeted with a huge sack of goodies that resembled trick-or-treat bags, only with all health foods. Beyond being spellbound by the massive provision of food at meals and for snacks, I walked away with two profound observations that are relevant to this section. First, the single word that best describes the tone or atmosphere of the experience is *serious*. The team members were not a bunch of college students having fun playing football. They were carefully selected, physically gifted, and highly trained, professional-acting students totally serious about their *commitment* to winning.

My second surprising major observation was that the guys on the team were not as big as I expected. Antonio Langham, an All-American cornerback and later first-round draft pick of the Cleveland Browns, was so scrawny-looking in street clothes that I thought he was one of the managers.

Then there was George Teague, a defensive back and later first-round draft choice of the Green Bay Packers who was famous for stripping the ball from Miami receiver Lamar Thomas sprinting for the end zone in the National Championship game. George was one of my students who came to class in shorts early in the semester when the weather was still balmy in Alabama. I had a simple reaction to George in shorts: *Buddy, I thought, you better do a lot of heavy weight lifting in the off-season or some 300-pound lineman blocking downfield is going to crush those twigs for legs.*

Finally, there was David Palmer, another student of mine. David was listed as five feet, nine inches tall in college, but apparently, he shrunk an inch after leaving college because the Minnesota Vikings had him listed as five feet, eight inches tall. Yet, as an underclassman at UA, he looked so small in street clothes that if he were to pick a fight with you, you would probably be too amused to fight or you would walk away out of pity. When a fight does break out, however, you had better make sure that David is on your team. David Palmer was an All-American, all-purpose athlete who finished third in Heisman balloting in 1993. He gives new meaning to the hackneyed saying that dynamite comes in small packages.

Ultimately, that 1992 National Championship football team comprised of ragtag runts and a rancher for a coach was a unique confluence of highly committed followers. "Brother" Bill Oliver, the Crimson Tide's defensive coordinator, was so moved by the commitment of this team that he claimed, "We had guys that would run through hell in gasoline underwear."

Committed Follower Compatibilities

Any leadership style, culture, or climate may be compatible with your committed followership style (1) depending on the object of your commitment and (2) as long as the object of your commitment is optimized or uncompromised. For example, a follower committed to management out of appreciation for caring about its employees would obviously fit best in a people-oriented organization. However, if your commitment is to the organization's clientele, you may be content with either a bureaucratic culture or an autonomous climate depending on which one serves the clientele optimally. Given that the basis for organization commitment is frequently the mission of an organization and because they tend to maximize the achievement of organizational missions, high-learning and task-oriented organizations that focus on the customer are most compatible with committed followers.

None of the organizational cultures and climates in table 6.1 jump out as being highly incompatible with your committed followership style without knowledge of additional variables that might moderate the climates and cultures. And all of the leadership styles, cultures, and climates can be the nemesis for committed followers if they interfere with the object of your commitment. However, in the absence of complete moderating information, the bureaucratic culture has the highest probability of interfering with your commitment if bureaucracy is true to its reputation of creating red tape that interferes with the achievement of goals and missions.

Conforming Follower Compatibilities

Every spring semester, I have my students fill out a questionnaire that determines whether they would best fit in the general civil service as employees hired because of their qualifications or the career civil service as employees hired because of their potential to develop in an occupation that lasts throughout a career. I am amazed at the high percentage of students (typically around 30 to 40 percent) who are interested in the career civil service until they find out that the most well-known career civil services are the armed forces as well as police and fire departments. Yes, those of you who are conforming followers are well suited for these military and quasi-military organizations. With the necessity for disciplined teamwork to provide optimally efficient operations during times of war, raging fires, and lawlessness on the streets, military-like leaders and cultures demand compliance and respect for authority that is highly compatible with the nature of conforming followers. Don't panic. Any organization culture and leadership style that emphasizes teamwork, such as other career civil services like the Foreign Service, Coast Guard, and Forest Service, would also be compatible with your conforming followership style.[6]

Because you are willing to comply with centralized decision-making, as well as with environments heavily reliant on rules, you also fit well in bureaucratic cultures and structures. In turn, given that conformists typically have a need to be accepted and appreciated, people-oriented leaders and cultures should also be appealing to you because they reinforce that conformists fit in and are valued. Even if you do not fit initially, people-oriented leaders and cultures care enough about conformists to help them discern how to conform and belong. As a conformist, you are typically the most tolerant follower of autocratic leaders, and you will likely thrive to conform to the desires of charismatic leaders.

Conformists are least compatible with innovative and creative cultures and climates, as well as transformational leaders, because they necessitate thinking and behaving in unconventional, nonconforming ways. Laissez-faire leaders can sometimes be a bad match because they do not provide conforming followers much that they can conform to. Research laboratories, think tanks, the arts, entertainment, and new product development divisions typically require too much independent and flexible thinking for those of you with strong natural needs to conform. Organizations that exist in rapidly changing environments—brokerage houses, emergency rooms, commodities exchanges, athletic teams—can also be problematic for conformists because what they are conforming to is frequently a moving target.

Practical Follower Compatibilities

The leadership styles, cultures, and climates in figure 1 that embrace democratic principles are the most compatible with your practical followership style because they provide a check on unrealistic or extreme actions that have a greater probability of occurring in autocracies and oligarchic leadership teams. Laissez-faire leaders should also appeal to you because they give you the freedom to function according to your practical standards and methods. The safety climate is also quite compatible with your practical followership style because of its no-nonsense, levelheaded emphasis on the financial and physical security of its organization and employees. Moreover, ethical cultures and climates that are utilitarian would also appeal to you because they do not lock you into ideal standards that can be too difficult for most humans to realize; plus, they emphasize a commonly accepted and understandable principle of making decisions that bring about the greatest good for the greatest number of people.

In contrast, because innovation and creativity are fed through pushing people's imaginations to extremes, they might cause some of you to feel as though you are working in a looney bin. Unchecked autocracies also allow for actions that can violate your sense of practicality unless the autocrat is a practical leader who exercises better practical judgment than the collective wisdom of the broader workforce. Organizations that conduct themselves according to universal ethical principles that are too idealistic and difficult to live up to would also be a poor fit for your practical tendencies.

Self-Oriented Follower Compatibilities

Do not feel guilty if you scored moderately high on self-orientation. Not everyone wants to be a minister, social worker, or scientist discovering the antibiotic to eradicate the Zika virus. Furthermore, every job that a person holds provides a service to humankind or else there would not be a demand for that job. With that said, the people-oriented organizations should appeal to your followership style because they focus on the care and nurturing of employees. Developmental cultures should also be appealing because they bring about growth in employees that allows you to earn promotions, acquire marketable skills, and feel more competent and confident. Laissez-faire leaders and autonomous organization climates are also attractive to self-oriented followers because they give you the freedom to perform your job in a manner that minimizes boredom, maximizes your interests, and plays to your strengths.

Less obvious, the entrepreneurial climate should also be attractive to you because of the opportunities to grow and develop as new goods and services and novel methods of operation are explored and cultivated. Of course, successful entrepreneurial climates are also appealing because of the financial windfalls that you can benefit from. Although some leadership styles, cultures, and climates may have a stronger likelihood of satisfying you than others may, any of them can be compatible with the needs of a self-oriented follower as long as they maximize your self-interests.

Likewise, any leadership styles, cultures, and climates can cause problems for the self-interested depending on the broader circumstances. Nevertheless, autocracy has the greatest likelihood of compromising your autonomy and therefore your level of job satisfaction. Ironically, democratic organizations can be off-putting to self-interested followers because they commonly require you to compromise, thus reducing self-control and the opportunity to maximize your personal interests. Ethical cultures and climates that hold followers to lofty standards can also be trouble because they demand self-control that inhibits your self-expression. Moreover, they often create formal and informal norms of behavior—red tape—that can cause you to be less efficient.

Conclusion

The single most significant point of this chapter is that you should affiliate with organizations that are compatible with your followership styles. Followership personalities are difficult to change, and we can make ourselves and those around us miserable when we are functioning in organizations that are incompatible with our natural followership styles. You must do your homework on organizations before you affiliate with them. Moreover, it is quintessential that you are highly reflective and brutally honest about who you really are before deciding to join a work, religious, civic, or social organization that may or may not be compatible with your followership styles. You may believe, for example, that being an independent follower is appealing and admirable, but do not deceive yourself by thinking that you are an independent follower when your behavior dictates otherwise. Furthermore, once in an organization, stay attuned to the leadership styles, culture, and climate in an ongoing assessment of your compatibility with the organization. And have the courage to find another job, join a different church, or drop out of a social organization that proves to be incompatible with your followership styles. Since finding another job can be difficult, finding the most compatible job in the first place is essential. However, sometimes switching jobs within an organization will do the trick if the switch allows you to work under a more compatible leader, subculture, or subclimate within an organization.

Let's turn to chapter 7 to explore your compatibility with the remainder of common followership styles that are opposite to those investigated in this chapter.

CHAPTER 7

More Follower Havens and Hades

Similar to instructions in chapter 6, unless you have a unique desire to learn about all followership styles, read only the sections of this chapter that pertain to your specific followership style as identified in chapter 5.

Passive Follower Compatibilities

If you are a passive follower, my fervent desire is to understand the reason for your passivity. My professional training tells me that your passivity is a symptom of a more fundamental cause rather than a statement about your basic nature. I align with scholars who contend that humans are naturally active, or what we call "intrinsically motivated."[1] Unfortunately, bad experiences often douse that spark of excitement for life that compels us to explore and experiment and to thirst for growth and development. Consequently, my assessment of your compatibilities will be contingent upon a perspective that accepts your passivity and another that believes that beneath your veneer of passivity is the active person that you are truly meant to be.

If you are a genuinely passive person, your followership style is most compatible with autocratic leaders and bureaucratic cultures and structures. In these conditions, your job is more reactive than proactive because decision-making power is hoarded by leaders in a centralized organization structure. You are able to act, yet only when instructed. In between instructions, you have downtime that should appeal to your passive nature. If you are chronically passive, a team or collaborative culture can also work to your advantage because the burden of work is shared, and you can shift a disproportionate amount of work to teammates through never volunteering for anything or by doing such a poor job on assignments that others do not want to give you any responsibilities. In fact, this last strategy was used by a nameless history professor at UA who was exceedingly bright, socially adept, and thus a seemingly attractive person to serve on important campus committees. Committed to his own research rather than the business of the university, he did what a lot of faculty only dream of. He purposefully came to meetings unprepared and participated with such an off-the-wall demeanor that he thwarted the capacity for others to get any work done. Suffering from the collegial equivalent of the bubonic plague, he was quarantined from serving on committees for most of his academic career.

However, I am not letting you off the hook by assuming that you are truly passive. And, if you are immutably passive, I need to warn you that being a bad teammate to satisfy your passivity has its downside. Social rejection, a bad reputation, poor pay raises if the boss catches wind, et cetera, all should be weighed against your passive proclivities. Instead, I believe a better choice than a team culture would be an autonomous work climate because you have the freedom to perform your job when you have the most energy and motivation. More importantly, you have the freedom to do your job in a way that brings you the greatest stimulation and satisfaction. If the autonomous climate is paired with an independent job so that you are not inconveniencing teammates with your sporadic spurts of motivation, even better.

Yet, the best choice of compatible organization types is based on the assumption that you are actually a motivated human being who is experiencing passivity because your job is not stimulating or meaningful. If you are the under stimulated passive follower, you are most compatible with cultures and climates that emphasize continuous development of new knowledge, skills, and abilities. Innovative, entrepreneurial, and creative cultures and climates also demand new ways of thinking about your work products and processes that can give new life to passive followers stuck in the doldrums of growth-depressing jobs. For some of you who are working in jobs where you are removed from your clientele, a customer or service organizational climate might rekindle your active nature. Through putting you in direct contact with customers or making you more aware of customers, such climates reinforce your importance to others. Realizing that you make a difference in the lives of others should evoke positive feelings and a motivation to sustain those feelings through ongoing service to your clientele.

Now, if you are a demotivated follower with a stimulating job that has caused burnout, then your needs are different than the under stimulated passive follower. The type of leadership style, culture, and climate that will best respond to your passivity reflecting burnout is clearly the caring, people-oriented organization because its members are disposed to recognize your burnout, to own up to the organization's contribution to your burnout, and to take action to restore your psychological health and intrinsic motivation.

If there is nothing that can rekindle your motivation, your passive followership style is most incompatible with task-oriented organizational environments where there is substantial pressure to produce at high levels. Organizations that emphasize learning and development, participation, and entrepreneurialism demand a level of activity that is also inconsistent with your passive nature. By contrast, if your passivity is a symptom of a curable cause, autocratic leaders and dominant cultures are diametrically opposed to the fundamental nature of the active person—the real you—hiding beneath a veil of passivity. Bureaucratic cultures with their red tape and centralized decision-making are also inconsistent with the true active you.

Alienated Followers: Can They Be Redeemed?

In September of 1976, I walked into a college classroom on the south side of the University of Georgia campus to teach the first 30 of over 6,000 college students whom I have taught in my career. Although I was eight years older than my students, my boyish looks, no doubt, were confusing because I could easily pass for an upperclassman that had flunked Political Science 101 as a freshman and was returning to earn passing credit as a junior or senior.

As I surveyed the class for the first time, I recall thinking that there was nothing unusual about the physical appearance of the students with the exception of a young woman dressed in black, looking like what baby boomers would call a "hood." Today, you might describe her appearance as a cross between a Goth and a thug. Her demeanor was also consistent with her appearance in that she copped a sarcastic, recalcitrant attitude and seemed to enjoy harassing the mammoth football player who sat at the desk in front of her. In goading a jock, I interpreted her behavior as showing contempt for something as conventional and popular as college football in the SEC.

Realizing that I needed to do something to modify her class behavior, I proceeded with a principle and approach that I always start with in dealing with classroom problems. The principle is simple: solve the problem in the least painful and most face-saving way possible. Moreover, the first step is something that you have likely heard more than once in life—kill them with kindness. Now, you might think that killing someone with kindness is a wimpy way to solve problems, but I think that it is both genius (turning enemies into allies) and usually much more difficult to do than losing your temper, casting aspersions, or threatening people. Regardless, did the approach work?

I made a point of bumping into my black-clad, contemptuous student after class in order to initiate a conversation. I have no recollection of the content of the conversation that occurred 37 years ago, but I recall the overall tone being surprisingly more positive and pleasant than I had anticipated. A couple of weeks later, I inadvertently bumped into the same student at a Halloween party. We talked and talked and laughed a lot, especially at me who had tripped and landed in the apple-bobbing bucket on a crowded apartment balcony. But again, did my approach change the student's classroom behavior? Absolutely. Not only that, the soft problem-solving approach allowed me to make a cool new friend—a gal who looked like she had just walked off a stage production of *Grease*!

A Potentially Alienated Follower

After four delightful years teaching at Texas Tech University in Lubbock, Texas, I started to become uneasy with the isolation of Lubbock given that it was six hours by car to the nearest major metropolitan areas— Dallas, Texas, and Albuquerque, New Mexico. I loved living in Atlanta, Georgia, in the mid to late 1970s and wanted to return to a culturally enriched city with professional sports teams, and an abundance of young professionals. Consequently, I accepted a job at California State University, Fullerton (CSUF), located in a bedroom community of Los Angeles.

Anyone who moves to Los Angeles fast learns that "laid-back" Southern California is a myth. The area is too congested, polluted, crime-ridden, and unaffordable for most people to enjoy any semblance of the easy-going life that may have existed in the first half of the 20th century. Most notably, Southern California is too competitive socially, educationally, and especially professionally for most people to survive the environment with a carefree attitude. Moreover, for the first time in my teaching career, I experienced some consistently mean-spirited students, the most and least professional behavior that I have ever known, and the most saintly and morally depraved people in my life. I also observed indifference on scale that I had never witnessed before. Unlike Texans and Georgians, a critical mass of Southern Californians seemed incapable of taking simple delight in the fascinating mosaic of people that you find in a cosmopolitan city such as LA. I recall parties where I met no one and parties where I met people who always had somewhere else to go or something better to do than enjoy the current party. Moreover, holding a PhD and being a professor did not seem to impress anyone.

On good days, LA was heaven on earth; on bad days, I was convinced that the devil had succeeded in disguising hell as paradise. The competition and stress of living in metropolitan LA polished the halos of the best and sharpened the horns of its worst inhabitants. By the end of my first year in Southern California, I concluded that the mean-spiritedness of some and the indifference of others were different manifestations of the same thing—alienation. I also concluded that there were a handful of alienated students in my classes that I could never reach—they were alienated followers beyond my capacity to affect them. Yet, there was one student, whom I will refer to as John, who was not yet alienated but particularly vulnerable to becoming alienated, at least from the Master of Public Administration (MPA) program at CSUF.

John was one of the brightest graduate students in my classes. A gentleman in his demeanor, he was quieter than his classmates but more thoughtful and poignant whenever he spoke. I was very impressed with John and therefore shocked when he did not pass his comprehensive examination—the final hurdle for completing his MPA degree. John broke the only commandment that can cause a bright, prepared student to fail a "comp": Thou shalt not drift off topic. He wrote an extremely thoughtful and well-documented answer to a question that was not asked.

Imagining that John was upset and believing his failure was a fluke, I took him aside to explain what had happened and to give him a pep talk. Above all, I wanted him to understand that he was extremely bright, that he would never repeat the error that he had made when he took his comps, and that I had no doubt that if he retook his comps a semester later, then he would pass with flying colors. And that is exactly what happened.

However, what was particularly profound to me was the story that he shared after he passed the comps. John told me that he had been a gang member growing up in Southern California. He was alienated by the system and acted with impunity to the point where he was in and out of trouble with the law. He proceeded to tell me that three people in his life believed in him. None of the three included his parents. John had a parole officer who never gave up on him. Plus, he fell in love with a woman who brought out the best in him—a woman who was such a kind, decent, and loving person that he wanted to be a different man in order to be worthy of her love and the quality of life that she offered him. To my great surprise, the third person that he felt believed in him was me.

Now, I don't claim to have a halo shining over my head, but if I do, it is tarnished beyond recognition. However, John shared that he might not have had the confidence to retake and pass his exams without receiving encouraging words and reassurance of his talent. He could have easily returned to old, alienated tendencies if he had not been reassured of his talent.

If I told you that my soft approach in dealing with alienated students always worked, I would be lying. However, I can say that the soft approach has worked for me 95 percent of the time and that the alienated follower is most compatible with caring, people-oriented leaders, cultures, and climates.

The Pygmalion Effect: Self-Fulfilling Prophecies

My experiences with John made me very aware of the veracity of what the management literature calls the Pygmalion effect. Pygmalion was a mythical Cypriot sculptor whom the Roman poet Ovid wrote about in an amazing 15-book narrative poem titled *Metamorphoses*. Pygmalion sculpted a woman out of ivory who was so perfect in appearance that Pygmalion fell in love with her. In making an offering at the altar of Aphrodite, the Greek goddess of love, he secretly wished for a bride in the likeness of his sculptured beauty. He returned home to find that his sculpture had come to life.

In the management literature, the Pygmalion effect is best described as a positive self-fulfilling prophecy or, more specifically, an increased level of performance that occurs when leadership or management believe in and have high expectations of employees. The Pygmalion effect has been researched so extensively that major review articles have established that the effect is most likely to occur in men, in military organizations, and in people who have initial low expectations or low performance.[2]

Alienated Follower Compatibilities and Incompatibilities

Like the passive follower, I believe that your alienation is simply a symptom masking the committed follower lurking beneath the surface. I suspect that you have a laudable work ethic, so the negative reaction to the problems in your work environment is manifested as alienation instead of passivity. If your alienation is symptomatic of limited opportunities for self-expression, then laissez-faire leaders and autonomous climates will allow you greater freedom to be yourself. Moreover, innovative and creative cultures and climates will provide you broad latitude for self-expression that should help reduce alienation otherwise caused by narrowly defined jobs.

If the alienation is symptomatic of unjust treatment, then ethical climates and cultures as well as justice or fairness climates are compatible with your alienation because they are environments that have the greatest likelihood of preventing and correcting wrongdoing. People-oriented leaders, cultures, and climates are also inclined to be sensitive to your alienation and to correct the reason for the poor treatment whether it is inequitable pay, being passed over for promotions, bad work assignments, views not being heard or valued, an unsafe work environment, lack of recognition, et cetera. Often, a transformational leader will also address the causes of your alienation, especially if other followers share your alienation and the alienation is not based on selfish tendencies.

For the same reason articulated in the previous section on passive followers, autocratic leaders, authoritative or dominant cultures, and bureaucratic cultures have the greatest likelihood of being incompatible with your alienation. Empirical research also demonstrates that centralized hierarchies and formalization (job codification, rule observation, and job specificity)—characteristics of bureaucracy—increase work alienation.[3]

Individual Follower Compatibilities

Individual followers are quite varied by nature. They include introverts, highly focused hound dogs that are impervious to distractions, the artistic with such strong needs for self-expression that they can't work in groups, and those with strong needs for achievement who also don't work well in groups. Your individual followership style is most compatible with a laissez-faire leader, that is, a leader who is hands-off in her approach to managing you. Innovative and creative cultures and climates will also allow you the self-expression that you may desire, and you are highly compatible with autonomous climates because they give you the freedom to work independently.

Authoritative leaders and dominant cultures, in contrast, will be the bane of your organizational experience because they limit your discretion and self-expression. The centralized decision-making and authoritative exercise of power that is typical of bureaucratic cultures and organization structures will also impede your need for independent expression, as will the constraining rules and procedures of safety-oriented and rules-and-standards-oriented climates.

In closing, because you can be easily mistaken for someone who does not care about the organizations in which you are a member, pairing yourself with the right type of organizational leader, culture, and climate is more critical than you might realize. In turn, bosses who recognize your individualist nature and talent have the pleasure of going gleefully to their superiors with reports of your sterling performance knowing that they had to do absolutely nothing beyond accommodating your particular individualistic needs and setting you free.

Idealistic and Dreamer Followers: Troublemakers and Heroes

Dreamers evoke reactions ranging from celebration to castigation, especially if you're an active follower. When your vision differs from others' or requires sweeping change, you can become a stone in everyone's shoe. When your vision is on target but your capacity to sell it is two or three steps ahead of your colleagues, you may be an irritant producing a pearl, but to others you are just an irritant. Moreover, when your idealism is about means—how people conduct business—rather than ends, you can rest assured that you will peeve a large segment of coworkers predisposed to cut corners, fudge performance data, ignore the rules, and put themselves before the needs of the company and clientele. If you confront these problems publically, there is no telling how resentful and vindictive humiliated colleagues can be.

As a dreaming follower, you're also the muse and energy for a more meaningful, productive, enjoyable, and exciting organization. Your vision inspires others to noble ends, and your idealism sets an example that rouses others to a higher standard of behavior. When your dreams are shared incrementally and with clarity and diplomacy, you are well down the road to becoming a major change agent in your organization. Pair this behavior with a vision that captures the dreams of others and the know-how of practical followers, and your dreams become realities.

Dreamer and Idealistic Follower Compatibilities

As a dreamer, your followership style will flourish in innovative and creative cultures and climates. There your dreams will be encouraged and developed without the judgment and obstruction from leaders and followers who are passive, overly practical, or defensive of the status quo. Moreover, your dreams and ideals have the greatest likelihood of coming to fruition in innovative and creative cultures. Although you will inevitably share dreams that do not have enough appeal to be realized, they will not be judged harshly, nor will you be discouraged from developing and expressing them. While laissez-faire leaders will also give you the freedom to pursue your dreams and ideals while fulfilling your job responsibilities, transformational leaders who share similar dreams and ideals will be the most copacetic match to your followership style.

Most learning cultures and climates should also provide a nice fit for your dreams and idealism because they are all about developing analytic skills, evaluation capacities, and creative abilities leading to more optimally operating organizations.[4] Organizations with cultures and climates emphasizing highly ethical behavior are also likely to appeal to your idealism. Just make sure that you conduct an investigation thorough enough to determine whether the ethical standards of your organization are consistent with your own ethical standards.

In contrast, autocratic leaders and dominant cultures are far too controlling to free you to pursue your dreams and ideals, even if they serendipitously share your dreams. The centralized decision-making endemic to bureaucracies will also inhibit your capacity to pursue dreams and ideals, as will the strict adherence to rules and standardized procedures that protect people and institutions in safety-oriented cultures.

A Little-Known Altruistic Follower

Unlike Mother Teresa, Martin Luther King Jr., and Albert Schweitzer, Toyohiko Kagawa is a relatively unknown 20th-century humanitarian whose recognition slips through the cracks largely because of his Japanese heritage and anti-Japanese sentiments during and after World War II.

Kagawa was born to a wealthy, philandering father and a concubine who both died when he was four years old. While living with an uncle, he decided that he wanted to learn English and received instruction from two missionaries who ran a Christian school in Kobe, Japan.[5] Learning English through reading Biblical scriptures, Kagawa found a theology that he loved, and he consequently converted to Christianity at age 15.

His love for Christianity eventually reached such depths that he felt called to enroll in the Kobe Theological Seminary and thereafter move into the slums of Kobe to begin his mission to serve the poor. In the slums of Kobe and later Shinkawa, Japan, Kagawa's acts of selflessness became legendary. In Shinkawa, he rented a 90 square-foot windowless shelter in an alley. Yet, on an income of only $10.50 per month, Kagawa housed and fed himself and three otherwise homeless men—a murderer suffering from mental illness, a man covered with syphilis sores, and a jobless man with a skin disease with whom Kagawa shared his bed and subsequently contracted his disease.

During another period, he spent every cent of his meager income to lodge, feed, and care for 16 sick people. A beggar once demanded Kagawa's shirt, pants, and coat. He faithfully obliged. Having no other clothing, he wore a bright red woman's kimono given to him by a former prostitute. Others mocked him for looking the fool. He lovingly agreed. The consummate altruistic follower of his religious faith, Kagawa served the poor and the laboring class through direct personal care of the sick and hungry, labor activism, and his prolific writing ability. He penned over 150 books, yet never hid behind his pen, as evident in his social activism that led to his imprisonment on three occasions.

Altruistic Follower Compatibilities

Your unselfish gifts of service to others are so profound and special that I cannot help but emphasize the importance of your followership style being placed under the right leadership style and right organizational culture and climate. Customer-oriented climates are the ideal match for your altruism, as are ethical cultures and climates that emphasize utilitarian values of doing the greatest good for the greatest number of people. Ethical cultures and climates with a commitment to social responsibility or Judeo-Christian love are also a strong fit for you. Justice and fairness climates are compatible with your altruism, as are autonomous climates and laissez-faire leaders because they give you the freedom to perform a job in a way that maximizes your other-orientation. However, laissez-faire leadership and autonomous climates are not enough for your altruistic nature. It is essential that your job be structured in a way that allows you either substantial direct contact with your clientele or substantial authority to make decisions that have a profoundly positive impact on the lives of others.

Bureaucratic and military cultures have the greatest potential for obstructing your altruistic proclivities because their hierarchies can insulate you from the clientele that you want to serve, and decision-making is too centralized and removed from frontline employees who know how to best help customers. Mindless compliance to bureaucratic rules can also displace otherwise altruistic organization purposes and lead to inflexibility and insensitivity to the true needs of clientele and colleagues that you desire to meet.[6] Unless a dominant culture is committed to altruistic ends, it too will corral your altruistic efforts through hoarding power and imposing a self-serving agenda.

As I close this section, I would like to pause to share with you, the altruistic follower, the tersest yet sincerest sentence in this book. Thank you. When life's difficulties become too knotted and overwhelming, you are our rock. You comfort us in our pain, you solve our problems, and you give us hope. You reassure us that there is still fundamental goodness in life, and your actions and example inspire us to be better human beings. If you are ever feeling lonely and unappreciated, dog-ear this page, highlight this paragraph, and read it over and over again. When life seems to be nothing more than an endless chess game of moves and manipulations to maximize power, possessions, and position, you are the rebel who refuses to play. Keep being that rebel. We need you more than you can ever imagine.

Conclusion

In chapter 3, we addressed the characteristics of followers that employers are looking for. To the extent that you can cultivate any of those qualities, terrific. However, chapters 4 and 5 assume that developing desirable qualities can be a challenging and time consuming endeavor for many followers. Given that there may be a large degree of constancy in your followership style, chapters 6 and 7 consequently encourage you to identify the organization cultures, climates, and leadership styles that best match your style. Identifying compatible employers is the next step, but the real work comes from ensuring that your qualifications are outstanding enough to land a job in the perfect organization for your followership style. If that requires that you finish your GED or a PhD with better grades than you ever made before, follow the Nike motto—*just do it*. If that means working longer hours, taking unappealing assignments, or traveling as part of your job in the short run, again, *just do it*.

One of the most meaningful principles in life that does not get enough attention in the personal development, self-help, and theological literature is the principle of delaying gratification.[7] Through making sacrifices now for the long-term goal of working in an environment that is compatible with your followership style, your occupation will eventually become a greater source of joy. If you are anything like the average employee in the United States who works 47 hours per week, you owe it to your psychological and physical health to work those hours in an environment that values your followership style and that you find fulfilling.[8]

CHAPTER 8

Becoming a Satisfied Follower:
The Verdict of a Quarter-Million
Employees

When I think of quintessentially satisfied followers, every example that I want to share with you brings a smile to my face. As satisfied followers, they are so darn upbeat at work that their happiness is infectious. Take Steve Reed, a fellow professor whose teaching and research specialization is Japanese politics. I remember sticking my head in Steve's office one summer to make superficial small talk that included asking him where he was going on vacation. Totally preoccupied with his work and without taking his eyes off his computer monitor, Steve calmly replied, "I'm on vacation." I, in turn, noted, "Steve, you're sitting at your desk doing data analysis." Steve retorted, "Yes, and I love it."

One of the most satisfied and intrinsically motivated persons that I have ever known, Steve left The University of Alabama but not because of a bad experience. He was simply so enraptured by Japanese politics that he could never be totally satisfied unless he lived in Japan. For the last 20–some-odd years, Steve has served as a professor at Chuo University in Tokyo. Although he is well beyond retirement age, I suspect that he is sitting at his office desk this very moment conducting some arcane data analysis or reading some abstruse journal article and experiencing such great pleasure that he continues to think that he's on vacation.

Perhaps my favorite satisfied follower, however, is Tim Brando, the sportscaster for FOX Sports who is also well known for broadcasting college football and basketball for ESPN and CBS during his career. I met Tim when he was staying with my brother-in-law while he was in Athens, Georgia, to broadcast a University of Georgia football game on a sultry September afternoon in late the 1990s. The game had been so sweltering that we both took a dip in my brother-in-law's swimming pool after the game where we engaged in a postgame analysis. To my surprise and amusement, Tim talked about the game in a manner that sounded like he was still broadcasting the game. In fact, he came across a tad like Ron Burgundy, the parody of a news anchor in the movie *Anchorman* and *Anchorman 2*. But Tim was an intelligent Ron Burgundy and extremely engaging.

As I listened to Tim talk football, I came to a gleeful conclusion that Tim is the real deal—a man who genuinely loves football and talks about it in a natural or habitual vocal style that comes across as a television announcer. This was further reinforced by several interesting facts that I learned about Tim. First, he attended the University of Louisiana, Monroe, not an exclusive private university with an elite journalism or telecommunications and film program. Second, he does not run in the fast lane of sports broadcasters and journalists by residing in New York City or Los Angeles; he lives in his lifelong hometown of Shreveport, Louisiana. Finally, when I asked Tim, a man in his early forties at the time, where he wanted to go with his career, he did not understand the question, even after I posed it a second time. It became eminently clear to me that Tim was completely fulfilled in his status as a sportscaster. I say bravo to the person in CBS corporate headquarters in New York City for recognizing Tim's ability and venturing beyond the products of the leading broadcasting programs and the Manhattan-based broadcasting pool.

The body of research on what brings about job satisfaction is enormous and nothing short of exciting for those of us who like to discover and share findings. I was able to locate 46 meta-analyses—review articles that combine data from smaller studies to arrive at more statistically valid findings than the uncombined, aggregate findings from small studies. These meta-analyses present the collective knowledge from over a thousand studies on the job satisfaction of several hundred thousand employees. Nineteen of the meta-analyses address organizational factors that affect job satisfaction in a variety of organizations and occupations.[1] Eleven more meta-analyses address job satisfaction for specific occupations including nurse, salesperson, accountant, principal, school psychologist, employee of an educational organization, and information systems professional.[2] Finally, 16 meta-analyses address what you bring to organizations in terms of your nature and values and how that determines whether you will be a satisfied or dissatisfied follower.[3] However, let's first take a look at the meta-analyses addressing the organizational factors that bring about job satisfaction.

The meta-analyses reveal three variables and two organizational dimensions that subsume more than one variable that have a large effect on job satisfaction.

Organizational Experiences Having a Positive Impact on the Job Satisfaction of Followers

Job satisfaction increases when followers experience:

1. a well-designed job
2. a just work environment
3. management behaving with integrity
4. a good person-organization fit
5. a supportive organization

More specifically, well-designed jobs have a large effect on job satisfaction when they are clearly defined, challenging, and have a significant impact on the lives of others. A well-designed job also allows employees to work autonomously, complete a whole product or service, receive performance feedback, and use a variety of skills.

Job satisfaction also increases substantially as employees experience distributive, procedural, and interactional organizational justice. Distributive justice refers to the fairness of the allocation of outcomes such as pay raises and promotions.[4] Procedural justice refers to the fairness of the processes that determine outcomes, while interactional justice is concerned with the quality of interactions, especially the communication between management and employees.[5] For example, communication reflecting interactional justice leading to job satisfaction is respectful, honest, and polite.

Somewhat related to the justice and fairness experiences of followers are their perceptions of the integrity of management. "Management behaving with integrity" refers to the alignment between what management says and does.[6] When managers are true to their personal word and the principles of their organization, employee job satisfaction is elevated substantially.

Riggle et al.'s meta-analysis indicates job satisfaction elevates substantially when followers perceive that their organizations support them or "value their contribution" and "care about their well-being."[7] Finally, the meta-analyses reveal that the person-organization fit has a large effect on job satisfaction. The guru of person-organization fit scholarship, Amy Kristof of the University of Iowa, defines organization-fit as "the compatibility between people and organizations that occurs when . . . the organization and the individual contribute to the fulfillment of needs of the other . . . or the organization and the individual share similar characteristics."[8]

By contrast, the meta-analytic research also demonstrates that three variables and a cluster of two variables have a large *negative* effect on job satisfaction.

Organizational Experiences Having a Negative Effect on the Job Satisfaction of Followers

Job satisfaction diminishes when followers experience:

1. organizational politics[9]
2. role stress caused by role ambiguity and role conflict
3. management breaching a contract
4. nonsexual aggression[10]

Academics commonly define organizational politics as "self-serving work behaviors not sanctioned by authority" or the selfish scheming and maneuvering of employees outside the formal structure and policies of an organization.[11] While perceptions of organizational politics have a large negative effect on job satisfaction for all followers, sadly, they have an even stronger negative effect on the job satisfaction of ethnic minorities and international employees.[12]

Roles also have a large negative effect on job satisfaction when they are ambiguous and conflictual. Ambiguous, or unclear, roles cause confusion and uncertainty about how to act. Acting in the face of ambiguity enhances the possibility of making a poor choice about what to do, whereas not acting in the face of ambiguity can elevate anxiety for those wanting to act but not knowing what to do.

Role conflict occurs, in turn, when followers face incompatible demands in their jobs. For example, followers may experience dissatisfaction when feeling pressure from their immediate supervisors to produce at a higher rate, while at the same time experiencing pressure from the legal department or human resources to slow down and comply with various regulations and procedures that prevent product liability and employment discrimination lawsuits. Together, role ambiguity and role conflict bring about role stress, or perceptions of potential or actual threatening situations that diminish job satisfaction.[13]

The negative relationship between psychological breach of contract and job satisfaction occurs when people realize that an organization has failed to deliver in its obligations, such as failing to deliver an agreed upon salary, perk, workload, assignment, or job.[14] Finally, nonsexual aggression, defined as obstructionism and hostility, has a negative effect on the job satisfaction of men and an even larger negative effect on the job satisfaction of women. Aggression in the form of obstruction refers to acts that impede the capacity of an employee to perform her job, while hostile aggression involves acts such as "yelling, giving dirty looks, belittling someone's opinion, ignoring them, making negative or obscene gestures toward someone, spreading negative rumors."[15]

Organization-Related Predictors of Job Satisfaction in Specific Occupations

Research on specific occupations reveals nearly 60 findings relevant to what predicts job satisfaction. However, most of the significant findings are non-repetitive in that the different meta-analyses investigate different factors that affect job satisfaction. Regardless, certain job-related factors recur even in these reviews of research in very different occupations. If you consider empowerment, independent work, and control over your job as being synonymous with autonomous work, then job autonomy is the leading recurring organizational characteristic affecting job satisfaction in these very diverse studies on the subject. In turn, four different samples demonstrate that positive and collaborative relationships with colleagues and superiors have a positive impact on job satisfaction, as do considerate and supportive leaders and climates. By contrast, in four different studies, role ambiguity and role conflict reveal negative impacts on job satisfaction.

When you merge the organizational-related factors that lead to job satisfaction with those repeated by different professions, the factors leading to greater follower satisfaction do not change dramatically (see below). Job autonomy fits with the other factors relevant to a well-designed job, and supportive climate fits quite well with supportive organizations. Moreover, the large negative effect of role ambiguity and role conflict on job satisfaction surfacing in the studies of specific professions is entirely consistent with the findings from the studies on mixed professions.

Merged Organizational Experiences Having a Positive Effect on Follower Job Satisfaction

- A well-designed job (including job autonomy)
- a just and fair work environment
- a management team that behaves with integrity
- a good person-organization fit

- a supportive organization (including a supportive climate)
- positive relationships, including collaborative relationships (new to the list)
- considerate and supportive leaders (new to the list)

Please remember that the leading causes of job satisfaction and job dissatisfaction are the best generalizations in the absence of complete information about you. I will never forget my first graduate seminar in the spring of 1982 when I was teaching the importance of well-designed jobs. I was waxing eloquently about the significance of jobs being structured in a way that gives employees authority and autonomy, that makes a difference in the lives of others, and that have greater meaning because they allow employees to see a project or service from beginning to end. I thought that I would endear myself to my women students by complaining vehemently about the dehumanizing work and waste of talent that many college-educated women from my generation experienced as they got stuck in jobs as receptionists and secretaries, mindlessly typing or answering telephones all day. To my surprise, the first hand that went up in the seminar was that of a woman doctoral student who curtly informed me that she could type all day long and that it did not bother her a bit.

Let me also emphasize that you will have problems attaining job satisfaction if your natural followership style identified in chapter 5 is incompatible with the elements of the ideal job design for job satisfaction. Table 8.1 charts the specific followership styles that are compatible and incompatible with the job design elements that are leading causes of job satisfaction. As indicated in the table, skill variety can be problematic for those of you who have hound dog tendencies or like to stay focused on a singular task with singular methods. Jobs requiring skill variety are also potentially problematic for conforming followers, especially if the various skills necessitate behaving in unique, unconventional ways. Job designs and tasks that are challenging and provide performance feedback, in turn, are problematic to passive followers because the nature of the work requires exceptional effort, and the feedback shines a light on poor performance. Performance feedback can also be a problem for alienated followers if it reveals behavior that is at odds with the expectations of the organization.

To further help you discern where you are likely to be the most contented follower, we must also take a look at a series of meta-analyses that investigate the effects of personality traits that employees bring to organizations. Ultimately, based on your fundamental nature, some of you are blessed to be content in most work situations while others of you are destined to be unhappy no matter what organizations you join.

Table 8.1 Followership Styles That Are Compatible and Incompatible with the Elements of the Ideal Job Design

Elements of the Ideal Job Design	Compatible Followership Styles	Incompatible Followership Styles
1. Autonomy	Individualist (especially) and all other styles	
2. Skill Variety	Committed, Active, Individualistic	Conforming
3. Challenging (including full skill use)	Active, Committed	Passive
4. Performance Feedback	Altruistic, Pragmatic	Alienated, Passive

Note: Because autonomy gives the conformist the discretion to conform, a conforming followership style is not in the incompatible column. Passive followership could be placed in the compatible column if passivity is a symptom of unchallenging work. Alienated followership could be placed in the compatible column if the alienation is caused by invalid feedback or the absence of feedback.

Personal Traits and Demographics That Affect Job Satisfaction

I remember reading an article in the *Los Angeles Times* about how different people react to their jobs. One individual featured was a young man who worked in a tollbooth taking fees and making change all day. During rush hour, the constant flow of traffic kept the man very busy; at other times, the flow of traffic made the work very intermittent. In the eyes of some, the job during rush hour might seem to be stressful, mindless work, while the job during slow periods might seem to be boring, uneventful work. Yet, the young man loved the job, especially during the slow periods because he could spend his time singing and dancing in his tollbooth that was just large enough to allow him practice all of the new dance moves that he wanted to learn.

I also have two friends who have performed public defender work for individuals accused of first-degree murder. One friend took on a high-stakes case that was quite complex and challenging—a conviction more than likely meant the death penalty for his client. Ultimately, the nature of the case allowed my friend to experience what academics know to be the three critical psychological states for work motivation and job satisfaction: meaningful work, responsibility for the job, and knowledge of results.[16] In the process of winning the case, my friend literally saved the life of a human being, had sole responsibility for achieving this incredibly profound outcome, and grew tremendously from the experience. Although this case had all of the hallmarks of a great job, in the end, he vowed that he would never again serve as a public defender in a capital murder case—it was just too stressful.

Another friend, Joanne, cannot get enough capital defense work as she has helped over 100 impoverished defendants receive life without parole instead of the death penalty. The glint in her eyes and the conviction in her voice as she talks about her work with poor, death-row convicts is so inspiring that it makes you want to sign up to help on her next case. Moreover, what is so amazing about Joanne is that her capital defense work has not been her full-time job. Until retirement, she was a full-time faculty member in the School of Social Work at UA, and she conducted capital defense work on the side. Motivated by deeply held beliefs that the poor, too, deserve first-class legal representation, she finds the work to be fascinating, gratifying, empowering, and, above all, meaningful.[17] Here we have a different person with a different personality having an opposite reaction to the same kind of professional responsibility. Let's segue to address what research tells us about personal traits that affect job satisfaction.

The 16 meta-analyses on the personality traits, attitudes, and demographics that affect job satisfaction represent nearly 1,000 studies, samples, or data sets investigating over 200,000 subjects. Although some traits have a large effect on job satisfaction, a large effect does not mean that you are blessed to experience job satisfaction or doomed to experience job dissatisfaction all of your life. Personality traits having a large impact on job satisfaction still do not explain a majority of the variation in job satisfaction.[18] A trait effect is large relative to the effects of other traits and findings common to behavioral research. However, paired with the right or wrong organization factors, your personality idiosyncrasies can have a significant influence on your job satisfaction.

If we focus on traits that have large positive effects on job satisfaction, only four surface.

Employee Traits Having a Large Positive Effect on Job Satisfaction

- **Positive affect** is a "generalized sense of well-being" or "predisposition to experience positive emotional states."[19] Scholars identify two types of positive affect—affect that is a stable trait of humans and affect that is a function of one's mood and subject to change.[20]

- **Life satisfaction** is the subjective global evaluation of whether one is "content, satisfied, and/or happy about one's life."[21] It is a "cognitive assessment of satisfaction with life circumstances."[22]
- **Organization-based self-esteem** reflects employee "beliefs about their value and competence as organizational members."[23]
- **Sense of coherence** reflects a person's capacity to perceive stimuli as being comprehensible, making sense, and being manageable and controllable.[24] A person with a low sense of coherence would see the world as "incomprehensible, hostile, and absurd."[25]

In turn, the only trait surfacing as having a large negative effect on job satisfaction is *negative affect,* or dwelling on one's "failures and shortcomings." People with negative affect are "more likely to be dissatisfied with themselves and their lives" and to "experience dissatisfaction across time . . . regardless of actual conditions."[26]

What Do You Do with This Information?

The goal of this chapter is to help you become a more satisfied follower through exposing you to what we know from thousands of studies on several hundred thousand employees. If your current job is heavy on the factors having a positive effect on job satisfaction—a well-designed job, just work environment, supportive leaders and organizations, managers with integrity, collaborative relationships, considerate and supportive leaders, and good person-organization fit—I would think twice before leaving your current position. If your job is light on the factors having large negative effects on job satisfaction—organizational politics, role stress, breach of contract, and nonsexual aggression—I would also think twice before leaving. Moreover, if you are about to enter the working world, I would use these two lists as criteria to help you determine what jobs to apply for and what jobs to accept.

By contrast, if your job is short on the factors bringing employees satisfaction or heavy on the factors having a negative impact on satisfaction, then I would initiate one of four actions: find another job, begin pursuing education and training that will qualify you for a more satisfying job, endeavor to change your attitude toward work, or try to bring about change in your job or work environment. However, let's focus momentarily on trying to bring about change in your job and work environment before you abandon ship. You owe it to yourself and your superiors.

Seeking Change in Your Job

I am always amazed by the responsiveness of humans when confronted about problems respectfully. In fact, sometimes it is downright embarrassing what people will do for you when you are simply kind and appreciative. I will never forget how, as a senior in college, I approached a professor about dropping his course because I made the stupid mistake of trying to attend a James Taylor concert and cram for a midterm during the same night. Unwilling to take a "diet pill" (speed) to keep me up all night studying, I accidentally fell asleep around 2:00 a.m. and woke up an hour before the midterm, having studied only one-third of the course material. I promptly sprinted to the professor's office, told him my story, and asked him for his permission to withdraw from the class because I did not want to ruin my grade point average by failing his midterm. I also let him know how much I loved his class. He was surprisingly sympathetic to my irresponsible behavior and was so insistent that I take the midterm that I realized that he was signaling to me that my grade would turn out fine. Trusting him, I sat for the exam, and, sure enough, the major essay question on the exam covered the first third of the course. I never expected that kind of help, and, looking back, realize that I was given unfair advantage. But for the purposes of this paragraph, this was the first memorable observation of a phenomenon that I have witnessed throughout my entire adult life. When you show modest appreciation for or take moderate delight in a person, you will frequently get more than what you ask for if your request is reasonable.

If your job design or role is imperfect, my suggestion is to visit with your superior to talk about the possibility of having more autonomy, work variety, role clarity, or whatever would make your job more satisfying. Visit with the boss when you are emotionally calm and, preferably, in a good mood. When the moment avails itself, show genuine appreciation for something positive in your boss. If the appreciation is not genuine, forget it. Not only will you come across as patronizing and manipulative, you will likely undermine your credibility and capacity to get what you want. Of extreme importance, however, is something that is commonly forgotten when trying to bring about change for personal benefit—*establish the mutual benefit of the change*. For example, demonstrate that the job redesign will allow you to produce at a higher rate, improve the quality of your work, solve an office-wide problem, or relieve excessive burdens falling on the boss's shoulders.

If the obstacle to your job satisfaction is the way that your supervisor treats you, the preceding instructions continue to be relevant if you *trust* the boss will not take it out on you for confronting him. If you do not trust your supervisor, convey the information through an anonymous means. However, dealing with a problematic boss or an organization-wide problem requires a finesse that will be addressed in chapter 10. For now, my major recommendation is do not leave your current job without exploring the possibility of bringing about change that will enhance your job satisfaction.

Are there bosses who only respond to the squeaky wheels? Of course. Yet why start with a negative approach and attitude when you are just as likely or *more likely* to get the desired results from a softer approach? Moreover, being selective about when you go to the boss with a bucket full of criticisms and emotions is important. Negativism as a default approach will undermine your credibility during the rare times when the boss really needs to understand how upset you are. Moreover, a negative default approach to problem-solving establishes your reputation as a chronic complainer and usually limits your opportunities to be involved in important decision-making processes. Let's face it; people do not like to deal with negative individuals and, whenever possible, will exclude them from the formal and informal dynamics that are making a difference in your organizations.

Pollyannas and Chronic Complainers

If you are a person who naturally experiences positive affect, life satisfaction, organization-based self-esteem, and a sense of coherence, then you will likely have a greater tolerance for the factors that have a negative impact on job satisfaction. But do not let Pollyanna propensities prevent you from pursuing jobs characterized by experiences that will bring you the greatest level of job satisfaction. In turn, if you are disposed to have a negative affect, then pursue the jobs and work environments that will minimize your dissatisfaction, but do *not* allow the chronic complainer in you to reject a gift horse when you are blessed to have a well-designed job, a just work environment, supportive leaders, managers with integrity, and collaborative relationships.

CHAPTER 9

Extraordinary, Ordinary, and the Worst Jobs for Followers

Over the years, little has changed with respect to the naïve occupational ambitions of many college students. As seniors, they often are so immersed in the college experience that they are not quite ready to move on. Between having the time of their lives, wanting to go through one more football season, or having a girlfriend or boyfriend who is in a class behind them, they decide to stick around campus a little longer by trying to gain admission to a post-undergraduate program. With bad grades or a dislike for the hard sciences, they rule out medical or dental school and mindlessly apply to law school as though it is the only option for an advanced degree. With unimpressive Law School Admission Test (LSAT) scores and an undergraduate transcript full of Bs and Cs, thousands of such students throughout the country are routinely rejected by law school admissions committees needing no more than five seconds to size up their clueless applications.

Then there is the select group of students who actually make good grades and score high enough on the LSAT to gain admission to law school. Yet similar to the below-average student, law school is a default choice because hard science or the idea of being a doctor or dentist is unappealing. So off they go to law school with a limited sense of the typical law school curriculum and with perceptions of the legal profession based on made-for-television depictions of criminal law, which is just one of a possible 103 categories of law that I identified in a brief scan of the Internet.

What happens to this group of students who attend law school as a default option versus those who choose law school based on an in-depth understanding of the study and practice of law and a true passion about being an attorney? They either dropout, finish law school and pursue a career outside the legal profession, take a job as a lawyer and eventually change professions, or sustain a career in the legal profession and limit their opportunity to experience a more optimally fulfilling career. The most tragic situation occurs when really talented students who are marginally wed to the legal profession land high-paying appointments at leading law firms working 60 to 70 hours a week.[1] When this situation is paired with a spouse, children, a mortgage, car payments, and law school debt, individuals can get trapped in the legal profession with seemingly no escape without making huge compromises to the comfortable lifestyles afforded by their professions. Moreover, this is a story that can be told about a variety of professions that seduce humans with the allure of high pay and high status.

My point, here, is to exhort you to do your homework before pursuing a career or career change with a surface sex appeal that puts you on a detour from becoming a fulfilled follower. Furthermore, just as we know that an enormous body of research can inform us of the factors that bring followers job satisfaction, another body of research allows us to identify the most appealing jobs for followers. Let's take a look at that research.

CareerCast Rankings of the 20 Best Jobs

One of the most thorough evaluations of occupations is conducted by the personnel at CareerCast, an Internet site that helps job seekers prepare for the job market and find jobs. Using data primarily from the Bureau of Labor Statistics, they evaluate jobs using 24 criteria dealing with the quality of the work environment, pay, outlook for the future, and stress factors.[2] However, before I share the CareerCast findings, for fun, write down what you think might be the five leading jobs in their rankings.

Top-Five Most Highly Ranked Jobs

1. _____
2. _____
3. _____
4. _____
5. _____

My guesses would be federal agent (FBI, CIA, and NSA), professional athlete, think-tank scientist, entertainer, and architect. Given some likely sex-role socialization affecting my selections, I asked my wife to share what she believed would be the five leading jobs, and she guessed marketing and public relations manager, information technology professional, fashion designer, actor, and executive search consultant. Let's turn the page and see how we did.

Wow, if you are anything like my wife and me, your predictions were pretty poor. The CareerCast rankings in table 9.1 reveal that actuary, audiologist, mathematician, statistician, and biomedical engineer were the five most highly evaluated jobs in 2015.[3] If we look at a five-year average of job rankings, software engineer leaps to second place and dental hygienist becomes the fifth most highly ranked job.[4] Moreover, financial planners and university professors move up into the top 20 jobs, while economists drop out of the top 20. Given the hundreds of jobs that exist in contemporary society, all of the jobs in table 9.1 are elite in terms of their potential to allow followers to find meaning and security in their occupations.

Most notably, jobs involving numerical data and statistics are disproportionately represented in the top 20 best jobs in table 9.1, as are healthcare-related jobs. Computer-related jobs and, to a lesser degree, engineering jobs are also disproportionately represented. But what if you are not a numbers kind of person? I have two reactions.

First, I would not waste a moment of doubt thinking you are missing out if you genuinely dislike numbers. High-paying jobs that have enormous upsides, wonderful colleagues, job security, and an absence of stress will not override your distaste for numbers that are at the essence of these jobs. It is no different from someone's dislike for opera. Just because you have the honor of sitting next to George Bush or Barack Obama in the Kennedy Center listening to Pavarotti sing *La Bohème*, does not mean that you are going to enjoy the evening's entertainment any more than an opera lover who does not relate to country music would enjoy the Grand Ole Opry or Country Music Awards with the honor of sitting next to Carrie Underwood or Garth Brooks. You are simply putting lipstick and fine jewelry on someone's donkey.

Second, if your dislike for numbers is not that intense, these jobs are sufficiently attractive to merit some thoughtful reflection. Do you have problems with all forms of math or just that course in trigonometry that you disliked in high school? Is your distaste for numbers a function of bad experiences with a poor math teacher or two, or did you still dislike your algebra class that was taught by an award-winning teacher?

Table 9.1   CareerCast Top-20 Best Jobs

Year	Top-20 Jobs	Rank					
		2015	2014	2013	2012	2011	Five-Year Average
2015	Actuary	1	4	1	2	3	2.2
	Audiologist	2	5	4	6	9	5.2
	Mathematician	3	1	18	10	2	6.8
	Statistician	4	3	20	18	4	9.8
	Engineer, Biomedical	5	12	2	NR	NR	6.3
	Data Scientist	6	NR[a]	NR	NR	NR	ID[b]
	Dental Hygienist	7	6	6	4	10	6.6
	Engineer, Software	8	7	3	1	1	4.0
	Occupational Therapist	9	9	7	7	17	9.8
	Computer Systems Analyst	10	8	10	9	5	8.4
	Speech Pathologist	11	10	12	11	21	13.0
	Dietitian	12	11	16	17	25	16.2
	Network and Computer Systems Administrator	131	9	NR	NR	NR	ID
	Human Resources Manager	14	13	31	3	NR	15.2
	Economist	15	18	120	48	20	44.2
	Optometrist	16	14	8	12	27	15.4
	Physical Therapist	17	15	9	13	45	19.8
	Meteorologist	18	21	29	29	6	20.6
	Engineer, Petroleum	19	20	28	16	24	21.4
	(tie) Medical Records Technician	19	21	35	50	40	33.0
Best 20 Jobs Not Previously Ranked							
2014	University Professor	29	2	14	NR	NR	15.0
	Financial Planner	22	16	5	5	15	12.6
	Medical Laboratory Technician	34	17	72	NR	35	39.5

Year	Top-20 Jobs	Rank					
		2015	2014	2013	2012	2011	Five-Year Average
2013	Chiropractor	26	34	11	19	32	24.4
	Physiologist	64	31	13	64	48	44.0
	Veterinarian	48	51	15	21	65	40.0
	Pharmacist	27	33	17	14	36	25.4
	Sociologist	31	30	19	20	11	22.2
2012	Online Advertising Manager	NR	NR	NR	8	NR	ID
	Web Developer	36	28	24	15	44	29.4
2011	Biologist	48	46	70	27	7	39.6
	Historian	43	54	25	30	8	32.0
	Accountant	42	40	47	47	12	37.6
	Paralegal Assistant	36	35	41	49	13	34.8
	Physicist	21	22	21	25	14	20.6
	Philosopher	NR	NR	NR	NR	16	ID
	Parole Officer	NR	95	27	35	18	43.7
	Aerospace Engineer	NR	87	100	60	19	66.5

[a]No ranking
[b]Insufficient data
Source: See endnotes 3 and 4.

Overall, the rankings in table 9.1 surprised me with one relevant exception—only one of the most highly ranked jobs, human resources manager, potentially involves a leadership role. All the other highly ranked jobs are primarily held by followers. In contrast, I could not initially understand why only one of my five leading job selections made it to table 9.1. My surprise reinforced a lesson that I should have learned in 1970 as a sophomore in college, but instead, learned 19 years later while teaching Air Force officers in an off-campus doctoral program at Maxwell Air Force Base (AFB) in Montgomery, Alabama.

A Late Lesson about a Career Option

As a sophomore in college in 1970, I was having a hard time deciding on a major, so I took a series of interest examinations to help guide my decision. The tests identified psychology and political science as my favored disciplines and, to my amazement, also indicated that I should be a cadet. This made no sense. As a young adult during the Vietnam War protest years, I was typical of a lot of students who had a great disdain for the military. In reaction to our country's engagement in what many believed to be an unconstitutional war, coupled with our exposure to the carnage and casualties of the war that appeared on nightly television, my generation of baby boomers was estranged from the military.

Fast-forward 19 years. I found myself accepting a job as a faculty member at UA and agreeing to teach one course annually in an off-campus doctorate of public administration program at Maxwell AFB. Experiencing some residual resentment of the military, I took on the responsibility anticipating that the experience might not be positive. After all, I was now teaching military officers, including some that were veterans of the war in Vietnam that I had protested.

After jumping through some hoops to demonstrate that I was up to the task of teaching military officers, I realized that I was enjoying my experience at Maxwell AFB. In fact, I felt that I was a kindred spirit to the officers that I taught. They took their studies seriously, but not themselves. They shared a common bond of service to the country, worked hard and played hard, and knew when to put their noses to the grindstone and when to pause for a good laugh and some stress relief. All and all, there was an esprit de corps at Maxwell AFB that reminded me of the better football and baseball teams that I had played on and enjoyed so much as a youth.

In finding meaning and delight in teaching what I perceived to be a *team* at Maxwell AFB, I realized that the test that I had taken as a 19-year-old was correct—I should have been a cadet and served a tour of duty or two in the military. So, do not overlook an occupation that has the potential to bring you great joy and comfort. Peruse the occupational rankings in this chapter with an open mind and the motivation to dig a little deeper into learning about the highly ranked jobs. However, if you are a person who is not into data and tables, feel free to jump to table 9.6 that summarizes the findings from the next four tables.

U.S. News and World Report and CNNMoney Rankings of the Best Jobs

U.S. News also ranks jobs annually and uses a formula that considers current employment rates, projected employment growth, average salaries, and employee job satisfaction.[5] In 2015, their five highest ranked jobs were dentist, nurse practitioner, software developer, physician, and dental hygienist (see table 9.2). Moreover, nurse practitioner, physical therapist, computer analyst, and registered nurse are ranked among the top-10 jobs in four of the five years reported.

Of the 26 different jobs in table 9.2, several overlap with the jobs in table 9.1—dental hygienist, physical therapist, computer system analyst, web developer, occupational therapist, and financial analyst (semi-overlaps with financial planner). And if you are not into numbers, you are in luck. In contrast to the CareerCast rankings, only two jobs—database administrator and financial analyst—are quantitative by nature. Finally, with the exception of 2011, a majority of the annual top-10 best jobs are medical or healthcare-related, and only one job in the entire table—education administrator—suggests a leadership role.

CNNMoney rankings in table 9.3 reveal a somewhat different set of jobs based on their promise for "big growth, great pay, and satisfying work."[6] In 2015, software architect, video game designer, landman, patent agent, and hospital administrator are the most highly evaluated jobs. The jobs ranking highly in table 9.3 are also not nearly as repetitive as those ranked highly over time by CareerCast and *U.S. News*. However, biomedical engineer, a top-five-ranked job by CareerCast, was the number-one-ranked job by CNNMoney in 2012 and 2013. The CNNMoney rankings overlap more with the *U.S. News* rankings in that both include dentists as a top-20 job in 2015. Software developer, database administrator, occupational therapist, physical therapist, and information security or assurance analyst are also found in the *U.S. News* and CNNMoney top rankings. Interestingly, only 10 of the 60 jobs in table 9.3 make the top-20 list more than one year. Moreover, software architect is the only job to make the top-20 list all three years reported.

A plurality (17) of the jobs in table 9.3 are healthcare-related, followed by 12 jobs that involve numbers (analysts, database developers, auditors, financial advisors), but these jobs are not as purely mathematical and statistical as the leading jobs of 2015 established by CareerCast. Computer- and IT-related jobs also demonstrate some repetition among the 50 different jobs in table 9.3. I suspect that you are starting to see some patterns of popular jobs at this stage, but the CNNMoney rankings take exception to the CareerCast and *U.S. News* rankings in that they include jobs that are not fundamentally follower jobs—for example, hospital administrator, auditing director, and pharmacist in charge.

Happy Jobs

Each year, CareerBliss, a "career community" dedicated to helping individuals find bliss in their employment, publishes the rankings of the

Table 9.2 *U.S. News and World Report* 10 Best Jobs

Rank	2015	2014	2013	2012	2011
1.	Dentist (3)	Software Developer	Dentist	Registered Nurse	Athletic Trainer
2.	Nurse Practitioner (2)	Computer Systems Analyst	Registered Nurse	Software Developer	Court Reporter
3.	Software Developer (4)	Dentist	Pharmacist	Pharmacist	Education Administrator
4.	Physician (3)	Nurse Practitioner	Computer Systems Analyst	Medical Assistant	Environmental Scientist
5.	Dental Hygienist (3)	Pharmacist (3)	Physician	Database Administrator	Veterinarian
6.	Physical Therapist (4)	Registered Nurse	Database Administrator (2)	Web Developer	Financial Analyst
7.	Computer Systems Analyst (4)	Physical Therapist	Software Developer	Computer Systems Analyst	Interpreter/ Translator
8.	Information Security Analyst	Physician	Physical Therapist	Physical Therapist	HVAC and Refrigerator Tech
9.	Registered Nurse (4)	Web Developer (3)	Web Developer	Computer Programmer	Public Relations Specialist
10.	Physician Assistant	Dental Hygienist	Dental Hygienist	Occupational Therapist	Radiologic Technologist

Note: Number in parentheses indicates the number of times repeated.
Source: See endnote 5.

A FOOTBALL PLAYER WITH A CALLING

A couple of years ago, a former student of mine renewed his wedding vows at Steadman Shealy's estate in Tuscaloosa, Alabama. Steadman quarterbacked the UA football team that ran a wishbone offense that was so prolific that they won the 1979 National Championship. The Shealys offered their home and hillside backyard overlooking Lake Tuscaloosa as a stunning backdrop for a sunset ceremony worthy of a cover for *Premier Bride* or *Wedding Style*.

I looked forward to visiting with Steadman because everyone who knows him always speaks so highly of his intensity, intelligence, and character. With an uncle and four cousins who played for Bear Bryant, I quickly dropped a couple of names to open the door to a conversation with Steadman.

To my great delight, Steadman did not disappoint. He was not only outgoing and engaging, but I also found him to be extremely down-to-earth for someone who was both a football legend and star in the legal profession in Alabama. But what was most fascinating about Steadman was that, unlike my nephew who was an attorney turned football coach, Steadman was a football player turned attorney. In fact, he felt called to be an attorney instead of pursuing professional football or a career in coaching. Whether Steadman's calling was an inner or external calling, I do not know. I was, however, convinced that Steadman was meant to be a lawyer, and, by the looks of his palatial estate on Lake Tuscaloosa, complete with horse stables and pastureland, he was, indeed, a successful lawyer.

Although I can, in good conscience, tell anyone that the job of an attorney has an average ranking, I can say with even greater conviction that, if you are *meant* to be an attorney, or any other particular professional, do not let anything stand between you and your calling. Heed the calling just as Steadman Shealy did!

10 happiest and 10 unhappiest occupations based on the reviews of 25,000 people who use their website.[7] Evaluating jobs using 10 criteria, CareerBliss site users reveal only a few similarities with the CareerCast, *U.S. News*, and CNNMoney rankings of jobs (see table 9.4). For example, the five leading jobs for 2015—school principal, executive chef, loan officer, automation engineer, and research assistant—do not appear in the other rankings, and only database administrator overlaps with *U.S. News* and CNNMoney rankings. Overall, 10 jobs in table 9.4 achieve

Table 9.3   CNNMoney 20 Best Jobs in America

2015	2013	2012
1. Software Architect (3)	1. Engineer, Biomedical (2)	1. Engineer, Biomedical
2. Video Game Designer (2)	2. Clinical Nurse Specialist	2. Marketing Consultant
3. Landman	3. Software Architect	3. Software Architect
4. Patent Agent	4. Physician, General Surgeon	4. Clinical Research Assoc.
5. Hospital Administrator	5. Management Consultant (2)	5. Database Administrator
6. Continuous Improve Mgr	6. Petroleum Geologist	6. Financial Advisor
7. Clinical Nurse Specialist (2)	7. Software Developer (2)	7. Market Research Analyst
8. Database Developer	8. IT Configuration Manager	8. Physical Therapist
9. Info Assurance Analyst (2)	9. Clinical Research Assoc. (2)	9. Software Developer
10. Pilates/Yoga Instructor	10. Engineer, Reservoir	10. Occupational Therapist
11. Clinical Application Specialist	11. Research Analyst	11. Management Consultant
12. Financial Advisor or Portfolio Manager (2)	12. Engineer, User Interface	12. Optometrist
13. Dentist	13. Hand Therapist	13. IT Consultant
14. User Experience Designer	14. Database Administrator (2)	14. Engineer, IT Network
15. Auditing Director	15. Video Game Designer	15. IT Security Consultant
16. Real Estate Development Manager	16. Telecommunication Network Analyst	16. Physician Assistant
17. IT Program Manager	17. Info Assurance Analyst	17. Construction Estimator

2015	2013	2012
18. Project Control	18. Bank Examiner	18. Personal Trainer
19. Specialist Pharmacist in Charge	19. Financial Advisor or Portfolio Manager	19. Employee/HR Trainer
20. Quality Assurance (QA) Coordinator	20. Compliance Manager	20. Engineer, Environmental

Note: Number in parentheses indicates the number of times repeated.
Source: See endnote 6.

top-10 status during more than one year, giving the CareerBliss rankings quite a lot of diversity in the types of jobs that are ranked.

The most common jobs receiving high happiness ratings are engineering jobs. Keeping in mind that the happiness rankings are based on the reviews of website users versus a random sample of reviewers and jobs, healthcare-related jobs are noticeably absent from the CareerBliss rankings. Moreover, depending on how you define leadership positions and whether the jobs have subordinates, a minimum of 6 and a maximum of 11 of the 40 jobs in table 9.4 would be considered leadership positions.

Finally, no review of the best jobs for followers would be complete without reporting the extensive work of Dr. Laurence Shatkin, the single most knowledgeable person writing on the nature and quality of different occupations. Evaluating jobs on their pay, growth rate, and position openings, Dr. Shatkin ranks jobs for different categories, or types, of people.[8] Table 9.5 presents his top-20 jobs for the 21st century, as well as the best jobs for introverts, college graduates, and people without four-year degrees. Application software developers, physicians and surgeons, system software developers, management analysts, and computer system analysts round out his top-five jobs for the 21st century. Management analyst is the only job in his top-20 rankings that has not been identified in at least one of the other job rankings in this chapter. In contrast to the CareerBliss ratings, Dr. Shatkin's rankings are much more similar to the rankings of CareerCast, *U.S. News*, and CNNMoney in his high rankings of healthcare- and computer-related jobs. His rankings also demonstrate a paucity of leadership-oriented jobs (two maximum) among his top-20 jobs.

The Consensus on the Best Jobs

Tables 9.1 through 9.5 and the rankings of the best jobs for women and the happiest jobs for young professionals identify nearly 200 jobs that

Table 9.4   CareerBliss 10 Happiest Jobs

Rank	Year/Job	Year/Job
	2015	**2014**
1.	School Principal	Research or Teaching Assistant
2.	Executive Chef (2)	QA Analyst
3.	Loan Officer (2)	Realtor (2)
4.	Engineer, Automation	Loan Officer
5.	Research Assistant (2)	Sales Representative (2)
6.	Database Administrator	Controller (2)
7.	Website Administrator	HR Manager
8.	Business Development Exe	Engineer, Software Developer
9.	Engineer, Software (2)	Intern
10.	System Developer	Team Leader
	2013	**2012**
1.	Real Estate Agent	Engineer, Software QA
2.	Engineer, Senior QA	Executive Chef
3.	Sales Rep, Senior	Property Manager
4.	Construction Superintendent	Teller
5.	Senior Application Developer	Warehouse Manager
6.	Logistics Manager	Administrative Assistant
7.	Construction Manager (2)	Customer Service Rep
8.	Administrative Assistant, Exec (2)	Accountant
9.	Engineer, Network	Engineer, System
10.	Controller, Assistant	Construction Manager

Source: See endnote 7.

have been ranked among the top 10 or 20 jobs by different evaluating organizations or individuals from 2011 to 2015.[9] I suspect that this might be a bit overwhelming to some of you, so let me pull together all of the rankings from the tables to see which 20 jobs are most frequently ranked highly. Moreover, all of you who are followers trying to find the right occupational fit for your nature should be sure to check out any number of Laurence Shatkin's several books that not only rank jobs, but also provide thorough job descriptions for every imaginable job that could ever kindle your curiosity.

Table 9.5   Twenty Best Jobs for the 21st Century, for College Graduates, for Those without a College Degree, and for Introverts

Best Jobs for the 21st Century
1. Software Developer, Applications
2. Physician and Surgeon
3. Software Developer, Systems Software
4. Management Analyst
5. Computer Systems Analyst
6. Nurse, Registered
7. Engineer, Civil
8. Medical Scientist (Except Epidemiologists)
9. Physical Therapist
10. Dental Hygienist
11. Accountant and Auditor
12. Network and Computer Systems Administrator
13. Pharmacist
14. Computer and Information Systems Manager
15. Physician Assistant
16. Market Research Analyst and Marketing Specialist
17. Construction Manager
18. Financial Advisor, Personal
19. Compliance Officer
20. Financial Analyst

Best Jobs for People without Four-Year Degrees
1. Nurse, Registered
2. Dental Hygienist
3. Construction Supervisor and Extraction Worker
4. Radiologic Technologist and Technician

5. Electrician
6. Plumber, Pipefitter, and Steamfitter
7. Construction Manager
8. Sonographer, Diagnostic Medical
9. Respiratory Therapist
10. HVAC and Refrigeration Mechanic and Installer
11. Sales Rep, Wholesale and Manufacturing (Except Technical and Scientific Products)
12. Sales Agent, Insurance
13. Physical Therapist Assistant
14. Brick Mason and Block Mason
15. Administrative Services Manager
16. Nurse, Licensed Practical and Licensed Vocational
17. Industrial Machine Mechanic
18. Business Operations Specialist, All Other
19. First-Line Supervisor of Helpers, Laborers, and Material Movers, Hand
20. Engineer, Operating Engineer and Other Construction Equipment Operator

Best Jobs for College Graduates
1. Engineer, Computer Software Applications
2. Engineer, Computer Software Systems Software
3. Computer Systems Analyst
4. Network Systems and Data Communications Analyst

(continued)

Table 9.5   (*continued*)

5. Financial Analyst	2. Engineer, Computer Systems Software
6. Sales Agent, Financial Services	3. Computer Systems Analyst
7. Sales Agent, Securities and Commodities	4. Network Systems and Data Communications Analyst
8. Health Specialties Teacher, Postsecondary	5. Accountant and Auditor
9. Computer Security Specialist	6. Lawyer
10. Network and Computer Systems Administrator	7. Financial Analyst
11. Management Analyst	8. Financial Advisor, Personal
12. Physician, Anesthesiologist	9. Medical Scientist (Except Epidemiologist)
13. Physician, Family and General Practitioner	10. Market Research Analyst
14. Physician, Internist and General	11. Engineer, Civil
15. Physician, Obstetrician and Gynecologist	12. Database Administrator
16. Physician, Psychiatrist	13. Cost Estimator
17. Physician, Surgeon	14. Plumber, Pipefitter, and Steamfitter
18. Computer and Information Systems Manager	15. Writer and Author
19. Financial Advisor, Personal	16. HVAC and Refrigeration Mechanic and Installer
20. Pharmacist	17. Environmental Scientist and Protection Technician, including Health
Best Jobs for Introverts	18. Engineer, Electrical
1. Engineer, Computer Software Applications	19. Graphic Designer
	20. Actuary

Source: See endnote 8.

Table 9.6 demonstrates that healthcare-related occupations and engineering jobs constitute nine of the top 20 best jobs. Engineer is the single most frequent highly ranked job, leading financial jobs by a wide margin. In addition to financial jobs, business-related occupations are well represented with actuaries, management analysts, management consultants, and *specific* types of sales representatives all landing in the top-20 best jobs. Computer-related jobs, including software- and network-related occupations, in turn, comprise 15.3 percent of the frequencies reported in table 9.6, while construction managers and supervisors, database developers

Table 9.6   The Twenty Most Highly Ranked Jobs

Occupation and Rank	Frequency Ranked Highly
1. Engineer, most commonly:	39
-Software-Related Engineer	13
-Biomedical Engineer	6
2. Financial Advisor, Planner, Portfolio Manager, or Analyst	14
3. Computer Systems Analyst	13
4. Dental Hygienist	12
Nurse, most commonly:	12
-Registered Nurse	7
Physical Therapist and Therapist Assistant	12
Physician	12
Software Architect, Developer, or Programmer; most commonly:	12
-Software Developer	8
-Software Architect	3
9. Actuary	9
Occupational Therapist and Therapist Assistant	9
Pharmacist	9
12. Medical Scientist, Technician, or Sonographer	7
Network Professional: Developer, Systems Administrator, or Systems Analyst	7
14. Construction Manager, Supervisor, or Superintendent	6
Database Administrator or Developer	6
Human Resource Manager	6
Marketing Analyst or Consultant	6
Optometrist	6
Sales Representative: Financial Services, Insurance, Securities and Commodities, or Wholesale and Manufacturing	6
Statistician	6

Source: See endnotes 4, 5, 6, 7, and 8.

and administrators, and statisticians constitute the remaining 8.6 percent of the frequencies in table 9.6. More importantly, any of the jobs in table 9.6 have the potential to bring you a satisfying, financially comfortable, and promising career in terms of the anticipated demand for the job.

Hopefully, there is a sufficient variety of jobs in table 9.6 to find something that appeals to you. Moreover, I would like to make two suggestions that are somewhat repetitive by now. First, if they do not outright repulse you, give some of the jobs in table 9.6 that are not your favorite a chance by taking a moment to learn about them. Second, if an occupation that does not appear in the tables and appendices in this chapter appeals to you without question—as your lifeblood, calling, or raison d'etre—feel free to finish reading this chapter with a confident smirk on your face or even a good laugh knowing that you have already found your occupational best fit. Last, let's not forget that this is a book on followership, and of the top-20 jobs reported in table 9.6, only construction manager or supervisor has leadership responsibilities for certain, while human resources manager and network administrator have formal leadership responsibilities if these positions have subordinates. Follower jobs are most consistently rated as the most appealing jobs by a variety of criteria and evaluators. So, what about the least attractive jobs? Let's take a look at two studies that may give you some direction on what to avoid.

The Lowest Ranked Jobs—The Obvious and Some Surprises

I cannot resist playing guessing games. It is a teaching habit used to engage students; plus, I am curious to know whether people perceive the world in a different manner than I do. So, in the space below, tell me what you think are the five worst jobs.

Your Top-Five Worst Jobs

1. _____
2. _____
3. _____
4. _____
5. _____

My guesses would be garbage collector, ditch digger, short-order cook, assembly line worker, and mover. Well, I am wrong again. How about you? CareerCast research reveals that, in 2015, the five worst jobs were newspaper reporter, lumberjack, enlisted military personnel, cook, and broadcaster (see table 9.7). Wait a minute; broadcaster and newspaper

Table 9.7   CareerCast 20 Worst Jobs

Year	Job Rank and Worst 20 Jobs	Rank					
		2015	2014	2013	2012	2011	Five-Year Average
2015	Garbage Collector	181	193	NR[a]	160	179	178.3
	Farmer (tied)	181	182	190	179	158	178.0
	Welder	182	185	NR	174	194	183.7
	Dairy Farmer	183	172	195	199	184	186.6
	Sales, Advertising	184	189	135	136	170	162.8
	Roofer	185	190	192	176	197	188.0
	Meter Reader	186	183	194	194	192	189.8
	Police Officer	187	187	166	163	178	176.2
	Buyer	188	167	177	146	156	166.8
	Flight Attendant	189	194	191	175	149	179.6
	Disc Jockey	190	188	179	180	177	182.8
	Mail Carrier	191	184	193	183	174	185.0
	Firefighter	192	192	167	185	176	182.4
	Taxi Driver	193	197	NR	187	196	193.3
	Corrections Officer	194	191	189	129	160	172.6
	Photojournalist	195	186	188	166	185	184.0
	Broadcaster	196	196	184	191	NR	191.7
	Cook	197	195[b]	NR	NR	NR	ID[c]
	Enlisted Military	198	198	198	198	NR	198.0
	Lumberjack	199	200	199	200	198	199.2
	Newspaper Reporter	200	199	200	196	188	196.6
Worst 20 Not Previously Ranked							
2014	Dockworker	179	181	178	165	NR	175.5
2013	Maid	128	118	181	182	169	155.6
	Butcher	169	179	182	192	182	180.8
	Fashion Designer	175	176	183	133	143	162.0
	Waiter/Waitress	171	174	185	195	139	172.8
	Tax Preparer	110	68	186	134	NR	124.5
	Dishwasher	129	124	187	193	167	160.0
	Oil Rig Worker	144	164	196	197	NR	175.3
	Actor	166	151	197	178	163	171.0

(continued)

Table 9.7   (*continued*)

Year	Job Rank and Worst 20 Jobs	Rank					
		2015	2014	2013	2012	2011	Five-Year Average
2012	Dressmaker/Seam-stress/Tailor	142	128	173	181	131	151.0
	Shipping/ Receiving Clerk	107	111	165	184	130	139.4
	Conservationist	87	53	133	188	72	106.6
	Drill-Press Operator	164	146	NR	198	154	165.5
	Shoemaker/Repairer	NR	NR	NR	190	145	167.5
2011	Plasterer	NR	NR	NR	NR	181	ID
	Auto Mechanic	176	173	102	145	183	155.8
	Child Care Worker	161	164	137	159	186	161.4
	Sheet Metal Worker	159	160	NR	150	187	164.0
	Sailor or Seaman	NR	159	163	152	189	165.7
	Stevedore	NR	NR	NR	NR	190	ID
	Construction Worker	157	161	171	173	191	170.6
	Painter	154	156	174	168	193	169.0
	Emergency Med Tech	173	NR	96	120	195	146.0
	Iron Worker	148	147	118	161	199	154.6
	Roustabout	NR	NR	NR	NR	200	ID

[a]No ranking
[b]Head Cook
[c]Insufficient data
Source: See endnotes 3 and 4.

reporter are bad jobs, as are photojournalist and disc jockey (the 6th and 11th worst jobs in 2015)? Covering breaking news and spinning the most popular music are bad jobs? And what about "be all that you can be" in the Army? Firing weapons, jumping out of airplanes, and flying helicopters all look pretty fun to me. But then again, these are superficial assessments based on limited exposure and little systematic investigation of these professions.

BROADCASTING JOBS—CELEBRITY STATUS WITH A COST

When I was on faculty at Texas Tech University in the early 1980s, I had a terrific time dating a woman who was a television reporter in Lubbock, Texas, and eventually a news anchor in Amarillo, Texas. Although covering the breaking news was exciting, the reporting job required her to be on call, work odd hours, and venture into some pretty seamy neighborhoods. While most people recognize that news anchors work unconventional hours in presenting the late night news or weekend news, I learned that, in small markets, anchorpersons write the news that they report and are under tremendous pressure to complete their stories in time to meet the deadlines of their next broadcast. Moreover, broadcasting jobs are in such high demand that television stations pay their employees peanuts. Coupled with the fact that broadcasters must constantly look over their shoulders for more pleasant voices or prettier faces that are willing to sell their children to get in front of the camera, these jobs are only attractive on the surface. My friend lasted two or three years in broadcasting before giving up her profession to become a flight attendant, also a low-ranking job, but not nearly as stressful and cutthroat as broadcasting jobs.

Most notably, 14 of the 20 worst jobs in 2015 involved manual labor, including 8 jobs that involved intense manual labor (e.g., lumberjack, roofer, garbage collector). The top-20 worst jobs in 2011, 2012, 2013, and 2014 that were *not* among the 20 worst jobs in 2015 were also overwhelmingly manual labor. Looking at five-year averages, taxi driver jumps into the top-five worst jobs, buyer and advertising sales rep drop out of the top-20 worst jobs, and butcher barely sneaks into the top-20 worst jobs.

Beyond the surprise of the broadcasting and journalism jobs ranking lowly, I was puzzled in learning that emergency occupations (firefighter and emergency medical technician), military jobs, and police officer positions are also ranked lowly. Saving lives, protecting the community, solving crimes, and ensuring the country's national security give these occupations a significance that clearly overshadows that of most jobs. They also appear quite exciting given the way they are depicted in television and film. But let's slow down. These jobs pay poorly, are physically dangerous, are highly intolerant of human error, and typically require people to work unpopular hours.

Research conducted by CareerBliss, in turn, reveals a different set of jobs that cause employees unhappiness (see table 9.8). They find that customer service rep, truck driver, technical support, legal assistant, and research analyst were the five jobs leading to the greatest unhappiness in employees in 2015. In contrast to the problematic jobs identified by CareerCast, CareerBliss reports *few* jobs that are blue collar and manual labor as the worst ten jobs between 2011 and 2015. Moreover, 13 of the 50 jobs listed in table 9.8 involve leadership responsibilities, and two more—product manager and program manager—may also if they involve the supervision of employees.

Prestigious Jobs and Winning at Following

Most of us like to feel important, and no doubt, having a job that allows us to experience status in the eyes of others can be awfully enticing. But are prestigious jobs quality jobs that, beyond satisfying our egos, bring us meaning and contentment? The final table in this chapter reports the top-10 most prestigious jobs reported in a Harris Poll of 2,537 adults. It also presents their rankings from the research conducted by CareerCast, *U.S. News*, and CNNMoney.[10] The data in table 9.9 most clearly suggests that, if you want to pursue a job with status, then avoid becoming a firefighter, police officer, or military officer, specifically a general. Instead, become a physician, scientist, or engineer—occupations that have high status but also consistently rank among the best 100 jobs. Although elementary school teacher is ranked in the bottom 100 jobs by CareerCast, preschool through high school teacher is also a prestigious job that otherwise consistently ranks in the best 100 jobs by *U.S. News*. Furthermore, recognizing that two of the seven rankings of nurses put them among the lowest 100 jobs, I am still inclined to encourage readers to consider a career as a registered nurse, nurse practitioner, or clinical specialist because their *U.S. News* and CNNMoney rankings are too high to ignore.

Confront Your Preconceived Notion about Jobs

One of the major roles of academia is to conduct research that reveals the error in our preconceived notions or that dispels the myths in the common knowledge that guides our daily lives. Hopefully, this chapter has achieved some of this end by demonstrating that some high

Table 9.8 CareerBliss Ten Unhappiest Jobs

Rank	2015	2014	2013	2012	2011
1.	Customer Service Rep (2)	Security Officer	Associate Attorney	Security Officer	Director, Information Tech.
2.	Truck Driver	Bank Branch Manager	Customer Service Associate	Nurse, Registered	Sales & Marketing, Director
3.	Technical Support (2)	Accountant	Clerk	Teacher	Product Manager
4.	Legal Assistant (2)	Customer Service Rep	Nurse, Registered (2)	Engineer, Sales	Senior Web Developer
5.	Research Analyst	General Manager	Teacher (2)	Product Manager (2)	Technical Specialist
6.	Clerk (2)	Sales, Executive/Director (3)	Marketing Coordinator	Program Manager	Electronics Technician
7.	Dispatcher	Technical Support Rep	Legal Assistant	Marketing Manager	Law Clerk
8.	Salesperson	Marketing Mgr/Coordinator (4)	Pharmacy Technician	Sales, Director (2)	Technical Support Analyst
9.	Merchandiser	Sales, Manager/Director	Technical Support Specialist	Marketing Director	CNC Machinist
10.	Security Guard (3)	Machine Operator	Case Manager	Maintenance Supervisor	Marketing Manager

Note: Numbers in parentheses indicate the number of times that the profession is ranked in the top-ten jobs over the years.
Source: See endnote 7.

Table 9.9   The 10 Most Prestigious Jobs and Their 2015 Job Rankings

Harris Poll Prestige Ranking	Ranking		
	CareerCast	*U.S. News*	CNNMoney
1. **Physician**	NR[a]	4/100	NR
-General Practice	83/200	NR	NR
-Surgeon	98/200	NR	NR
-Orthopedic Surgeon	NR	NR	33/100
-Anesthesiologist	NR	NR	36/100
-Psychiatrist	47/200	NR	NR
-Emergency Room	NR	NR	24/100
2. **Military Officer**			
-General	177/200	NR	NR
3. **Firefighter**	192/200	NR	NR
4. **Scientist**			
-Data	6/200	NR	NR
-Physicist	21/200	NR	NR
-Astronomer	25/200	NR	NR
-Sociologist	31/200	NR	NR
-Geologist	40/200	NR	NR
-Biologist	48/200	NR	NR
-Chemist	62/200	NR	NR
-Physiologist	64/200	NR	NR
-Anthropologist	72/200	NR	NR
-Archaeologist	73/200	NR	NR
-Zoologist	83/200	NR	NR
-Epidemiologist	NR	36/100	NR
5. **Nurse**			
-Registered	106/200	9/100	NR
-Licensed Practical	119/200	41/100	NR
-Practitioner	NR	2/100	NR
-Clinical Specialist	NR	NR	7/100
-Vocational	NR	41/100	NR
6. **Engineer**			
-Biomedical	5/200	NR	37/100
-Software	8/200	NR	NR
-Petroleum	19/200	NR	NR
-Civil	32/200	22/100	80/100
-Environmental	41/200	NR	NR
-Aerospace	55/200	NR	NR
-Industrial	65/200	NR	NR
-Mechanical	70/200	18/100	NR
-Nuclear	81/200	NR	NR
-Telecommunications			

Harris Poll Prestige Ranking	Ranking		
	CareerCast	*U.S. News*	CNNMoney
Network	NR	NR	39/100
-IT Network	NR	NR	71/100
-Transportation	NR	NR	89/100
-Technical Support	NR	NR	93/100
-Structural	NR	NR	99/100
7. Police Officer	187/200	NR	NR
8. Clergy	100/200	NR	NR
9. Architect	130/200	81/100	77/100
10. Teacher			
-Elementary	122/200	39/100	NR
-High School	NR	43/100	NR
-Middle School	NR	45/100	NR
-Preschool	NR	88/100	NR

[a]NR means "not ranked."
Source: See endnote 11.

A WRITER'S SOUL

In the mid-1980s, I went to lunch with a small number of political scientists and Lou Cannon, the senior correspondent to the White House for the *Washington Post* during the Reagan Administration. Having written five books about Reagan, Lou is arguably the world's foremost authority on President Reagan. It was fun to learn that, in contrast to all of the politicians that Lou knew, Ronald Reagan was the only one who espoused the same ideology off the record as he did in front of the camera. It was also fun to see Lou convince a skeptical team of PhDs that Ronald Reagan was a very bright president despite the fact that he was taking advice from Nancy Reagan based on the influence of an astrologer.

I was most impressed, however, in learning about Lou as a writer. While many children hide themselves under their covers with a flashlight and a comic book, Lou grew up hiding under the covers with paper, pen, and a compulsion to write. While storytellers are inclined never to let the truth get in the way of a good tale, Lou's behavior later that day spoke volumes about his basic nature and soul. Surrounded by attentive students and faculty who had brought him to campus as a special guest, Lou, unexpectedly, asked to be dismissed from the afternoon activities. His reason—he had to go write.

gloss-and-glitter jobs do not live up to their billing and that an ugly mutt can turn out to be the best dog-of-a-job that you will ever have.

As I close this chapter, however, I cannot help but reflect on my experience as an author writing this book. Every day, I look forward to conducting the research for this book because it allows me to learn something unexpected or intriguing about followers. And every day that I write, I look forward to sharing with you the knowledge that has brought me such delight. Yet, neither CareerCast, *U.S. News*, nor CNNMoney ranked author among their best 100 jobs in 2015. In fact, CareerCast ranked author 153 of 200 jobs in 2015. So, I repeat perhaps the most common half-principle that I teach in the college classroom—*in the absence of complete information, act on the best generalization* based on the facts such as those presented in this book. That best generalization is not to recommend that you or I become an author. However, the other half of that principle is that *in the presence of complete information, you can violate the best generalization.* With complete information, the ideal recommendation might be the exact opposite of your best generalization. For example, you might pursue a job as an author or any job with a low ranking because it is an occupational match made in heaven for you. Regardless, I hope this chapter makes us all a bit more curious and inclined to explore what our lives might be like if we pursued careers as engineers, financial planners, computer systems analysts, dental hygienists, physicians, software architects, or a dozen additional jobs that may be sleeping giants in their capacity to fill our souls in our follower roles.

CHAPTER 10

Overcoming the Unbecoming as Followers: Micromanagers, Passing on Bad News, and Unethical Bosses

"Some days you are the bug, some days you are the windshield."[1] This humorous metaphor falls short of the truth for a lot of us. In some dimensions of our lives, we are actually that crippled bug stuck on the windshield hanging on to dear life, not just some days, but day after day. This is reality in our lives as followers when we fail to act to rectify problems, which is too often a symptom of not knowing how to act. The goal of this chapter is to provide instructions on how to avoid the windshield, or, at least, how to bounce off the windshield with as little pain and injury as possible. This chapter addresses how to deal with three of the most common problems and challenges of followers: micromanaging bosses, sharing bad news with superiors, and unethical orders and assignments. Let's begin by addressing how to deal with that gnat swarming around you all of the time—the micromanaging boss.

How to Deal with Micromanagers

One of the most astute and humble actions we can ever take in life is to look at ourselves in the mirror and ask what we have done to cause or contribute to a problem. Likewise, a follower should start by critically examining whether he has done anything that is causing the micromanagement.[2] Has your work been completed on time, is it sufficiently thorough, does it do what your boss asks of you, is it communicated clearly, et cetera? Although discerning and correcting your responsibility for the micromanagement is the responsible action to take, don't be surprised if Big Brother's eyes are still all over your work. Micromanagement often has nothing to do with you and everything to do with your supervisor.[3]

I'll start with a firsthand example of a micromanager that I know well—me! Yes, guilty as charged in one dimension of my job. However, don't judge me or decide how to deal with me until you understand why. Why? Because that's what the experts would tell you to do in order to deal effectively with a micromanager.

Midway through my academic career, a graduate student of mine and I coauthored an article that we sent to one of the leading academic journals in my field. The article presented an unexpected research finding that ostensibly captured the curiosity of the editor and reviewers enough that they invited us to conduct some additional analyses and revise and resubmit the article for publication. Since my coauthor's full-time job was so demanding, I assumed the responsibility for conducting the new data analysis. Moreover, given that he had conducted the original data analysis, I did what most academics would do. I ran the original analysis again to make sure that I could reproduce his original findings before proceeding to conduct the new analysis. For the life of me, I couldn't reproduce the original findings.

Knowing that the coauthoring graduate student had never conducted data analysis for publication before, I concluded that his analysis was in error, corrected the error, and made sure that the journal didn't publish the surprising original finding that was not only incorrect, but also the exact opposite of the real story being told by the data. This experience reinforced the significance of closely monitoring the work of coauthors who are new to research and publishing in academic journals. That goal requires meticulous attention to detail that can only be taught through close supervision and abundant feedback that an outsider would likely label as micromanaging.

Understand Why the Boss Is a Micromanager

Through getting to know your supervisors and specifically inquiring about the broad reasons for their micromanagement, followers are in a better position to appreciate and realize the standards of a micromanager. Not only will the micromanagement feel more like help than meaningless intrusive behavior, meeting the boss's standard because you are genuinely committed to it will typically lead to the softening of the boss's micromanagement.

Ultimately, through getting to know your supervisor, you will likely learn that she is usually one of three types of micromanagers.[4] The following are the types of micromanagers, as well as their most and least compatible followership styles. The approaches to dealing with micromanagers have added significance if your followership style is incompatible with the micromanaging style of your boss.

Types of Micromanagers

1. **Anxiety-Driven micromanagers** are anxious due to enormous work pressures.
   a. Most compatible follower: active, committed, other-oriented
   b. Least compatible follower: passive, alienated, self-oriented
2. **Perfectionist micromanagers** have jobs or personalities that demand perfection.
   a. Most compatible follower: active, committed, other-oriented, idealistic
   b. Least compatible follower: passive, alienated, pragmatic, self-oriented
3. **Pathological micromanagers** have a need to control everything.
   a. Most compatible follower: passive, conforming, committed, other-oriented
   b. Least compatible follower: active, individualistic, alienated, self-oriented

The anxiety-driven and perfectionist typically respond positively to the same approaches to reducing their micromanagement. The pathological control freak, in turn, is largely a lost cause for reducing micromanagement unless you're a psychologist or psychiatrist with a lot of patience. However, you can minimize the anguish that a pathological micromanager can cause if you follow some significant rules presented in this chapter.

The ultimate solution to dealing with anxiety-driven and perfectionist micromanagers actually goes beyond learning, appreciating, and responding to their needs. The follower who develops the capacity to *anticipate and proactively prepare for their needs in advance* stands the best chance of bringing micromanagement to closure. So my advice to you is the following:

Stay a Step Ahead: Anticipate the Micromanager's Needs

I have no doubt that many of you are great parents who know your children so well that you can physically and metaphorically catch them before they fall. Good followers do the same with their micromanaging boss. The suggestion here is to know your supervisor's patterns and needs and the situations that trigger those needs well enough that you can predict and prepare for them.[5] If the boss has an important meeting coming up and you know that he will need an outcome assessment or a financial statement, have the information ready before he asks for it and thus avoid the nagging and meddling that comes when he has to initiate the request and anxiously wait for the documents.[6]

By habit, some people are consistently early, some are unfailingly late, and others are reliably on time in completing assignments. When dealing with a micromanager, you can dodge a lot of discomfort in becoming an early person because you have eliminated much of the need for micromanagement.[7] Send your boss whatever she needs early. Other than being chained to the necessity of being an early producer, you are free to plan, produce, and deliver your products and communications on your own timetable versus that dictated by the boss.[8] Look at your predicament realistically. Whether you are early, late, or on time, the demands of the job are the same, so why not become an early person who minimizes the gadfly qualities of your micromanaging boss?

Now if you are dealing with pathological micromanagers, then be prepared for a different reaction. The fact that you are competent enough to anticipate and provide for the boss's needs in advance may threaten him, as well as deprive him of a daily need to control you. There is no telling what kind of unwarranted demeaning reaction might be evoked without your exercising a masterful capacity for feigning humility and inflating the boss's ego with enough adoration to counterbalance the threat of your competency.

Keep the Micromanager in the Loop

As indicated, many micromanagers are victims of anxiety, and one of the leading causes of anxiety is the unknown.[9] Providing micromanagers with frequent updates of your activities and progress will allow them to refocus their attention on subordinates who are too clueless or resistant to meet their needs. Frequent updates also allow the micromanager "to address your questions, provide input, or suggest ideas . . . which will help her feel involved, yet prevent her multiple mid-day check-ins."[10]

Increase Trust through Consistency

The chains of micromanagement are eventually broken through demonstrating a consistent pattern of performance that meets the qualitative, quantitative, and timeliness expectations of your boss. That is, your boss will abandon micromanagement propensities when the acceptable level of performance becomes so predictable that she realizes it isn't worth the time to monitor your performance. The shackles will likely come off sooner if you have the talent, time, and energy to demonstrate a consistent pattern of *surpassing* your boss's expectations. Beware; surpassing expectations of a pathological micromanager can be ego threatening unless you can convince her that it reflects your submission to and adoration of her.

Flatter Your Way to Freedom

I cannot overemphasize the importance of acknowledging people for their talents and good deeds. Abraham Maslow, the father of need theories of human motivation, noted that only 10 percent of humans rise above their ego-esteem needs for praise and recognition.[11] Therefore, when superiors back off from their micromanaging tendencies, let them know how much you appreciate the freedom and how wise it was to let you operate independently.[12] Also, reinforce how impressed you are with your boss's talents, such as strategic planning, seeing the big picture, and advocating for your office, that aren't associated with getting caught up in the minutiae of your job. Finally, let the boss know that his administrative talents are far too valuable to be derailed with the details of your job.[13] Flattering a pathological micromanager, in turn, is a necessity for maintaining harmony in your relationship. Although you may not be able to flatter your way to freedom, you will reduce some of your manager's narcissistic need to tear you down to assert his self-importance.

Don't Fight Your Way to Freedom

Many of you have been taught that if you don't assert your needs in relationships, you will never get what you want. Moreover, confronting those who have power over you is often viewed as a venerable act of courage. Authorities concur that confronting a micromanager is an act of stupidity—a ready-made disaster that will inevitably backfire and make your situation worse, especially if your superior is a pathological micromanager.[14] The micromanaging control freak is predisposed to deduce that you are trying to hide something, can't be trusted, and, therefore, need even *more* micromanagement.[15] Forensic psychiatrist Roy Lubit further advises, "Don't try to show the boss [the control freak] the error of his ways. Don't criticize him or her. Don't try to point out mistakes or examples of unfairness. Avoid one-upmanship. All of these will lead to narcissistic rage and a blind desire to attack you. Above all, do not challenge their authority, power, or greatness. . . . Do not show off. Do not talk about your past accomplishments."[16]

Instead, you are to fall back on what I emphasized two paragraphs ago. Pathological micromanagers have serious self-worth problems that are best addressed by boosting their self-esteem through compliments, praise and recognition, and admiration.

Develop an Agreement Up Front

A final tactic to reduce micromanagement that is effective with some supervisors is to develop an agreement at the beginning of projects and assignments that establish the boss's degree of involvement.[17] Such an agreement will necessarily be contingent upon meeting the standards of your supervisor, and there is always the possibility that your supervisor will try to prescribe the process for achieving those standards. However, keeping your boss and the agreement focused on desirable outcomes instead of the means to the ends will buy you the operational freedom to complete a project in a way that enhances self-expression in work.

Move On

Authorities concur that there comes a time when you throw in the towel with micromanagers, especially those who have a pathological need to control you.[18] In fact, Lubit contends, "There is no chance that you will suddenly break through the psychological defenses of such managers and lead them to see the error of their ways."[19] When nothing seems to work or accommodating a micromanaging boss becomes too difficult, ask yourself whether it's worth the effort. All work environments have problems, and switching jobs often simply trades one set of problems for another. Instead of running from problems, we should often dig in our heels and learn how to solve or cope with the problems. The key, however, is doing enough homework to discern accurately whether the problems you encounter are more anomalous and destructive than what you could expect in any other organization. I strongly suggest calling on the wisdom of insightful coworkers, family members, friends, and professional counselors to help you discern whether to stay or leave your job.

My theological convictions lead me to believe that we have a responsibility to love everyone who touches our lives, and that includes the most difficult and despicable people we work with. Moreover, I observe too many people tapping out of relationships too soon, thus limiting their opportunity to develop deeper and more meaningful relationships, as well as more adept interpersonal skills. There are also people who lure us into games where we are challenged to solve the mystery of how to best love and get along with them. Yet the game is really just a scheme— a sting—to see how much emotional capital they can extort to solve a mystery that was never intended to be solved.

To be brutally honest, some of these people are smarter, more cunning, and more devoid of conscience than we are. They are simply too formidable a foe for us to believe that we can ever have a constructive, fulfilling relationship with them. Walking away from a pathological micromanager who fails to respond to your sincere, thoughtfully planned and executed efforts to realize a better working relationship is perfectly acceptable. To the extent that sparring with pathological micromanagers kills our spirit and diminishes our capacity to love others who need us and are more receptive to what we have to offer, the obligation to brush the dust off our feet and move on is no longer an option—it rises to the level of a moral imperative.

Delivering Bad News to the Boss

Passing on a thorough and timely account of bad news to a superior can be a frightening experience causing followers to dodge or procrastinate the responsibility, grossly understate the bad news, or even lie. Let me be clear. The consequences of getting caught succumbing to these avoidance behaviors are something to be more frightened of than the discomfort of reporting bad news. Beyond the punitive consequences that will eventually come and go, a superior's belief that you cannot be trusted can prevail through the lifetime of a relationship. So, how do you minimize the fear of passing on bad news and the negative repercussions of letting the boss know that you have a problem?

One of the most astute approaches for dealing with bad news is to have an ongoing relationship with your supervisor that includes a continuous flow of positive information. In essence, through keeping your boss apprised of the good things that you have done, as well as the good that she has done, you have already applied an anesthetic that lessens the impending pain that comes when bad news finally takes it turn.[20] By contrast, if your default pattern is to go to the boss only when you have problems, then you have inadvertently lowered your superior's threshold for pain and stacked the deck in favor of a negative reaction to the bad news. The key to further reducing the discomfort of passing on bad news and subsequent negative reactions is to have a well-laid and well-rehearsed plan for when to approach the boss, what to say, and how to say it.

The question of when you present bad news begs a two-fold answer. First, you present the news as soon as you recognize that there could be a problem, or, if the problem is unanticipated, as soon as it is recognized. Let's hypothesize that extenuating circumstances are likely to hurt your sales quota for a month. If your boss has an advanced heads-up on the specifics of the extenuating circumstances, he will come down on you substantially less hard than when you present unexpected bad numbers at the end of the month.[21] If a problem is unanticipated, such as sending a customer the wrong order or accidentally offending a major customer, don't wait a week to go to the boss. Go as soon as humanly possible, of course, after you pause to prepare your plan for addressing the boss.[22] Even if your procrastination is born out of fear and embarrassment, the odds are that your clientele and the boss will still see your delayed behavior as a sign of disrespect and insensitivity to their needs. Promptly fessing up to the problem, in turn, has the added benefit of reducing festering worry and anxiety that so often eats away at our emotional well-being while we procrastinate.

Second, you present the bad news when your superior will have the time to focus on your full story. When I was in my early 20s, I stewed over a problem for a month before I approached my boss about it. I then knocked on his door during the busiest time of the day while he was on the telephone. I then proceeded to share my problem while his telephone contact was put on hold. Needless to say, the outcome of my procrastination and bad timing was disastrous.

My advice is simple: Visit the boss when the time is convenient for her, not you—typically through an appointment. Or, drop in when the demands of the workday have slowed and she has quality time to spend with you.[23] Implicit in this advice is a person-to-person visit versus e-mailing, texting, or telephoning. Face-to-face communication allows the added benefits of vocal inflections and body language, as well as immediate feedback and the opportunities for clarification, elaboration, and the correction of misunderstandings.[24] In contrast to in-person interactions, e-mail, and especially a text message, will rarely capture the depth of one's sorrow, the sincerity of an apology, and the conviction of one's desire to make things right.

As for the content of your conversation with the boss, sharing the mitigating circumstances or difficulties that prevented you from being able to do what your superior expected is essential.[25] Explain why you missed a deadline or why a major customer is livid. Provide data—for example, evidence that an important delivery arrived a week late or was incomplete—that validates your explanation for the problem. If a disgruntled customer was out of line and others witnessed the bad behavior, then report their accounts or bring a colleague to a meeting to corroborate your side of the story.[26] You always have greater credibility when citing others or being accompanied by colleagues. Just make sure that your corroborating sources are people who are respected and trusted by your superior. Finally, the content of your meeting should *always include solutions* to the problem that you identified and an apology and acceptance of responsibility when you are genuinely culpable for causing the problem.[27]

The content of what you say and do in a meeting where bad news is shared is also driven by the dynamics of the meeting. You always need to adjust your tact based on how your superior responds to what you are saying.[28] If more information is requested, provide what's available or follow through on a promise to secure more information. Most importantly, give your boss a full opportunity to vent emotions and to let them subside while you remain calm. Venting may manifest itself in an outburst or the opposite—clamming up in a depressed silence.

To establish empathy and help turn emotions toward a productive conversation, Patterson, Grenny, McMillan, and Switzler (2002) in their *New York Times* Best Seller, *Crucial Conversations*, encourage you to paraphrase the boss's story, use mirroring language, and express agreement with whatever you genuinely agree with. In using mirroring language, for example, you acknowledge that the boss seems upset, angry, confused, or withdrawn.[29] To facilitate a constructive conversation when your superior acts withdrawn, Patterson et al. encourage you to "prime" the boss by voicing your best guess as to what he might be feeling.[30] Finally, when the boss attributes a problem to the wrong cause, including your incompetency or neglect, you are to compare the differences in your views, while never suggesting that the boss is wrong![31]

One of the more interesting debates about passing on bad news is whether to share good news or bad news first. The commonly espoused advice and practice is to sandwich the bad news between reports of good news, but research demonstrates that recipients prefer to hear the bad news first.[32] When the good news is presented first, people are inclined to anxiously await the bad news and are less likely to hear the good news. Beyond reducing worry, presenting the bad news before the good minimizes negative outbursts and gradually increases positive mood, as moving from negative to positive information appeals to human desires for a happy ending.[33]

In summary, the discomfort and negative consequences of going to the boss with bad news can be ameliorated through (1) a year-round habit of passing along good news; (2) a well-rehearsed plan of when, what, and how to approach the boss; (3) a thorough explanation of the causes of the problem; (4) providing solutions to the problem; (5) adjusting your approach based on the boss's reaction; and (6) presenting the bad news before the good news.

Dealing with Unethical Superiors

If you haven't already dealt with unethical colleagues and superiors, you are either amazingly lucky or extremely naïve. We are typically surrounded by employees who routinely exaggerate or lie about their sales or productivity numbers, use sick leave to take vacations, hire less-qualified friends in violation of equal employment opportunity, steal from their employers, falsify travel vouchers, and misrepresent income to avoid taxes. Moreover, one of the most emotionally, intellectually, and morally taxing situations that can beleaguer your life occurs when someone with power over you gives you an instruction to do something unethical. So, what do you do? Most people do nothing; my answer—*do something*. The reason you do something is because complying with unethical instructions from your superior leaves you too vulnerable to serious negative consequences if you get caught. On one extreme, you see employees being fired, fined, or imprisoned if the ethical violations are serious. Those that dodge the punitive extreme, however, can still permanently stain their reputation for integrity and trustworthiness and thus blunt their opportunities for promotions and desirable new assignments.[34] Even if there are zero negative repercussions, doing nothing or complying with unethical directives can lead to chronic guilt, emotional duress, anxiety over the need to do something, and depressing self-judgments about one's character.[35]

The consequences of reporting unethical behavior, refusing to conform to unethical group norms, or saying no to the boss's unethical instruction, in turn, can be equally devastating. The insidious reality is that you can be fired, labeled a troublemaker, marginalized, threatened and intimidated, denied promotions and pay raises, and given the worst assignments in retaliation for doing the ethically correct thing.[36] So, the questions is, how do you deal with unethical behavior at work in a way that minimizes the possibility of the vile retaliatory behavior?

The answer to that question depends on several factors: the seriousness of the unethical behavior, the time needed to expunge the organization of the unethical behavior, and your level of trust in your superiors and colleagues.

Create a Win-Win Situation through Education and Training

Richard Nielsen, professor of organizational studies at Boston College, believes that the solutions to ethical problems in organizations too often target individuals for their bad behavior in ways culminating in exonerations or punitive measures that devastate relationships and damage the organization.[37] Such targeting creates a win-lose situation that can be avoided if the ethical problems of your organization are not on the brink of being exposed and demanding that heads roll. Nielsen suggests that, with time and a modicum of leadership ability, individuals desiring change should proceed as team players offering to lead an effort to educate others through various forms of training and programs designed to inculcate new values and behaviors that change the organization's ethical culture. To enhance your credibility and capacity to persuade management to buy into this win-win approach, it always helps to bring in others who agree that problems exist and that education is an appropriate corrective measure. If management has trepidations, Nielson suggests one of my favorite tricks to keeping a great idea moving forward—ask to do a trial run with some element of your organization. Unfortunately, without time, upper-level support, or a receptive culture, a win-lose approach to addressing ethical problems is sometimes the only option.

Utilize Anonymous Sources When Trust Levels Are Low

If you want to destroy a relationship and create a permanent enemy, go to a person's boss or a policing authority instead of the employee and complain about her unethical behavior. So, why would you report someone's problematic behavior when a simple one-on-one interaction could resolve the problem, avoid punishment and retaliation, and save someone's face? The answer: you don't go directly to the alleged perpetrator when you don't trust her, especially when that person has power over you. Trust level always determines the degree of intimacy versus anonymity of an intervention to bring about change, and a person-to-perpetrator approach is not wise if you believe that it will lead to any of the negative repercussions already addressed.

Table 10.1   Where to Report Unethical Behavior When Trust Levels Are Low

Internal Sources	External Sources
• The perpetrator's superior[a]	• Attorney general
• A higher, more neutral superior than the perpetrator's boss[a]	• Perpetrator's professional association (e.g., bar association)
• Ombudsperson or inspector general's office	• State ethics commission
• Human resources department	• Union
• Legal department	• Regulatory agencies (e.g., EPA, SEC, EEOC, FINRA, OSHA, FED, FDA)
• Quality control	• Watchdog groups (e.g., PIRGs, NOW, NAACP, ACLU, BBB, Greenpeace)
• Sexual harassment officer	• Law enforcement agency (police, FBI, DEA)
• Suggestion boxes, hotlines, feedback surveys, and other anonymous mechanisms	• Media

[a]Use these sources only if you feel secure that they will not violate confidentiality.

When trust levels are low, you have lots of internal and external places where you can report unethical behavior (see table 10.1). If you want to minimize the turmoil, pain, and inconvenience to your colleagues, employer, and self, I suggest that you stick with reporting your concerns to an internal source, as well as exercising the procedural protocols (e.g., grievance procedures) laid out by your employer.[38] If you believe that shareholders or taxpayers have a right to know what is going on in your publicly owned company or government agency, reporting unethical behavior to an external source is also an appropriate action.

My first obligation is to keep you out of the quicksand of unethical behavior and, once in it, to get you out as quickly and injury-free as possible. That is why I recommend reporting unethical behavior to an internal official whom you *trust* to maintain confidentiality. Doing so covers your metaphorical backside. However, when the problem is serious, such as a potential felony violation, reporting the incident to an authority required to investigate and take action is essential not only to bring the perpetrator to justice, but also to ensure that harsh judgments aren't made about your character for failing to report a serious crime.

Let me pause, however, to encourage you to consider more than self-preservation in dealing with unethical behavior. Protecting others from being victimized by the unethical behavior of your colleagues and superiors is always a noble motive. Altruistic motives not only stand the test of time in the courtroom of public opinion, they also typically pacify a struggling conscience. Your altruistic motivations, however, can cause you to take aggressive actions, resulting in highly undesirable short-run consequences, such as being intimidated, ostracized, and denied promotions and pay raises. So, let's now look at how to minimize negative repercussions when you feel obligated or safe enough to address unethical behavior without hiding your identity.

How to Address Unethical Behavior When You Are Powerless and without Anonymity

Make Yourself Indispensable and Employable Elsewhere

You put yourself in a safe position to address superiors about unethical behavior through being an indispensable subordinate.[39] You become indispensable through having skills that no one else possesses in your organization or performing common skills at such a high level that management would be foolish to do anything that might cause you to leave. Developing indispensable skills also allows you to possess an exit plan to employment elsewhere in the event that confronting an unethical boss or colleagues becomes an untenable situation.

Have Plenty of Social Capital in Your Employer's Bank

You are also in a better position to voice concerns about unethical behavior when you are a superb subordinate, especially a team player with a large organizational social network. Management should be able to recognize that you are not a chronic complainer. Instead, you want to have a reputation throughout a broad social network for highly professional work, taking on unappealing assignments, volunteering for projects that add to your workday, and being there for colleagues and superiors in hard times. With a large deposit of social capital in the currency of goodwill in your company's bank, you earn the right to raise your concerns and have them be taken seriously without the fear of retribution.

Get Your Emotions Tight, Your Facts Right, and a Team to Support Your Position

Being pushed into the polluted waters of someone's unethical scheme can detonate an emotional bomb rather than douse its fuse. While they play well in movies and television, emotional outbursts rarely play well at work or in our private lives. Feelings and emotions need expression, and outbursts, without a doubt, get people's attention. My best generalization, however, is not to express and act on emotions when you are dealing with the object of your anger or ethical issues. Until they are under control, emotions can cloud our judgments and almost always dissuade others from wanting to deal with us. And, candidly, your unchecked emotions will cause a lot of people to think that you're just plain nuts.

Once a cooler head prevails, you must determine whether there is enough substance to your claim to justify reporting an ethics violation. When that discernment isn't clear, seeking the advice of people you respect both inside and outside the organization can be invaluable. In situations when insiders and outsiders disagree, I am inclined to side with respected outsiders because they aren't invested in the organization, don't know the players, and can therefore render a more detached and objective opinion.

If your homework persuades you to move forward with reporting the behavior, the details of the alleged unethical behavior must be carefully documented.[40] In order to build your case and bolster your credibility, it also helps to identify the company policy, ethics code, or law that you believe is being violated.[41] Credibility, in turn, is further enhanced through addressing the unethical behavior with a cadre of support from witnesses and victims of the unethical behavior, as well as with concerned colleagues.[42] The latter is where you can reap the benefits of having a social network built through your helping hand, good deeds, and professionalism.

Never be surprised, however, when fellow followers sympathize with your concerns but refuse to be a part of a show of force, especially against anyone whose power they fear. Also, don't be surprised if higher-level members of your social network fail to come through with support beyond their sympathy and advice. The sooner that we accept the fact that most people are conflict averse, the faster we can rid, forgive, and relish—that is, rid our ourselves of the disappointment, forgive those whom we can't rely on, and relish those gems who join us in our foxhole ready to take on the fight.

Be a Diplomat—Communicate with Savoir Faire and Solutions

Early in my career, I went to a boss and got him to admit that an assignment he had given me was unethical. Not smart. He became angry and defensive and ultimately refused to consider me for a different position that I was angling for. If I could relive the situation, I would take the advice that I am offering you now.

To begin, I would have addressed the boss on a day and at a time when he was in a predictably good mood and not too busy. I would have couched my concerns from the perspective and attitude of a team player, committed to the organization and the particular outcome of the assignment. Next, I would have brought the boss some options that would achieve his desired result in a way that best protected the organization, which would have been expressed as my primary motive. For example, I would have let him know that there was a reporter floating around our office asking lots of questions and that I had options that would eliminate the risk of the reporter writing an article that could damage the reputation of our organization. The content of the conversation would not have included calling my superior unethical, and I would have minimized my use of the word "problem." Instead, I would have focused on the benefits of the different options that I was offering. The icing on my agenda would have been to reinforce how much I loved working for him, which I did, and to praise the boss with sincere compliments for what he did well and what he valued.

This diplomatic approach can be summarized as follows: (1) address superiors when the time is conducive to a thoughtful, constructive conversation; (2) share your views from the frame of reference of a highly committed team player; (3) avoid criticizing (instead, share deserved compliments); and (4) bring solutions to the table that have a greater benefit than the ethically questionable assignment.

Concluding Thoughts for Unethical Situations

Most followers are too fearful to report unethical behavior, and those who aren't typically report the problem and take no further actions. However, if you are the type of person who wants to end unethical behavior, my advice is to solve the problem in a way that minimizes the pain and humiliation of the perpetrator. After all, why punish a person for their imperfections when solutions may be as simple and civil as sharing instruction and expectations about how to behave.

My advice is to start with your softest approach to dealing with the unethical behavior and take incrementally more aggressive steps until the problem is solved. Hopefully, you will never reach the point of having to hire a hitman! Don't be surprised, however, when your most civil approaches still bring extreme reactions. Most often, your civility will minimize ill will and facilitate resolution. It will also establish your reputation as a person of principle with the character to take action and solve problems in a way that maintains everyone's dignity. Behaving as such in an era when camera-happy characters appear more interested in name-calling than problem solving, you will be a scarce precious commodity—more than a diplomat, more like a godsend.

In chapter 11, I'll address how to deal with two more particularly challenging and perverse problems that followers usually experience at some point in their careers—sexual harassers and abusive, bullying bosses.

CHAPTER 11

More Overcoming the Unbecoming: Sexual Harassment and Abusive Bosses

Sexual Harassment

If you never reach out to hold a person's hand, extend a hug, or ask that special someone for a date, Cupid's arrow remains forever in its quiver as you deny yourself the need for affection and physical intimacy that is so fundamental to human nature. *But boy is it stupid to pursue that need in the work environment!* Unless a work-related romance leads to a successful marriage, there is inevitably a break-up, a termination of physical intimacy, and a desire by one party to continue physical intimacy, thus providing all the ingredients necessary for one ugly sexual harassment saga. My suggestion: when it comes to tending to your carnal callings, don't be lazy or restrictive. Beyond the dozen or so people in your office, there are several billion other people in the world with whom you could pursue physical intimacy.

Types of Sexual Harassment

Many of you already know through training that there are two types of sexual harassment. First, there is quid pro quo harassment involving favors such as pay raises and promotions in exchange for sex and penalties for denying someone sex. Second, the more common form of sexual harassment is a hostile work environment that occurs when employees are offended by unwanted verbal or physical behavior of a sexual nature. With two exceptions, the causes of a hostile environment are also fairly

Table 11.1   Recurring, Unwelcomed Behavior Constituting a Hostile Work Environment

• Sexual propositions	• Sexual questions
• Requests for dates	• Stalking a person
• Excessive flirting	• Staring or leering at a person's sexual regions; eyeing from head to toe
• Attempts to kiss someone	
• Touching: patting, rubbing, massaging, pinching, fondling, or leaning on someone	• Sexual comments about a person's body, including rating a person's body
• Sexual gestures, motions, and sounds (whistling, pelvic thrusts, kissing motions and sounds, or lip licking)	• Displaying or sharing sexual pictures
• Sexual jokes and teasing	• Words such as "darling," "sweetie," and "honey" used in a patronizing way
• Sexual letters, emails, phone calls, and texts	
• Suggestive language and innuendos	• Derogatory *sexist* language, including name-calling and nicknaming
	• Derogatory comments about a person's sexual orientation or gender identity

Source: See endnote 2.

well-known and can be found in Table 11.1.[1] People often do not know that derogatory *sexist* language, such as calling someone a bitch, whore, or slut is sexual harassment, as is derogatory language aimed at humiliating people because of their sexual orientation or gender identity.[2]

Employees are also sometimes unaware that their employers are legally liable for sexual harassment, and having grievance procedures and antidiscrimination policies is often not enough to avoid liability.[3] When I say that employers are legally liable, I mean that victims of sexual harassment can secure punitive damages from their employers unless they make reasonable efforts to prevent and promptly correct harassing behavior.[4] Moreover, not only do employers have a responsibility to try to prevent sexual harassment perpetrated by superiors, colleagues, or subordinates, they also have a responsibility to protect employees from clientele and customers who are harassers.[5]

Followers often assume a number of conditions must be met to qualify for sexual harassment, when the reality is just the opposite. Let's take a look at the unnecessary and necessary conditions for sexual harassment.

10 Unnecessary and Necessary Conditions for Sexual Harassment

1. Failure to say "no" and voluntarily responding to someone's sexual advances does not negate a claim of sexual harassment.[6] If sexual advances are unwelcomed, you have experienced sexual harassment.

2. You do not have to demonstrate psychological harm, impaired job performance, or loss of economic benefits to be a victim of sexual harassment.

3. You do not have to be harassed to be a victim. If you observe or learn about the sexual harassment experienced by a coworker, you can initiate charges against a harasser.[7]

4. Your use of foul language, occasional sexually explicit language, and sporadic sexual innuendo can add to the messiness of a sexual harassment claim, but such language does not invalidate your right to be protected from unwelcomed sexual harassment.[8]

5. A delayed sexual harassment claim is not a dead claim. Legal proceedings will likely need an explanation for the delay, but the courts recognize that the fear of repercussions and other circumstances may prevent victims from coming forward immediately.[9]

6. Your inability to produce an eyewitness to a sexual harassment claim does not defeat your claim. A courtroom decision will hinge on your credibility versus the credibility of the defendant.[10]

7. First-time, nonphysical incidents causing a hostile work environment are typically not considered sexual harassment because they do not reflect a pattern of harassment.[11]

8. "Unwelcomed, intentional touching" in "intimate body areas" is usually found to be sexual harassment, even though it may be a first offense.[12]

9. An organization can be liable for a hostile work environment even if offensive language and behavior does not target a specific person.[13]

10. When reasonable women find behavior toward a woman to be hostile and offensive, a man is guilty of sexual harassment, even though reasonable men might disagree.[14] The courts take the position of the reasonable women when a woman files a claim and the perspective of the reasonable man when a man files a claim.

How to Deal with Sexual Harassment

Any effort to address sexual harassment needs to begin with an understanding of what constitutes sexual harassment and how to file a sexual harassment complaint. The web links for the Equal Employment

Opportunity Commission (EEOC) and Merit System Protection Board (MSPB) citations found in this chapter are superb places for gathering this information by simply typing "sexual harassment" into the search function of their websites. If you work for a large organization, your employer should also have printed and electronic information available through its human resources department and legal department. Moreover, these departments typically have individuals who can counsel you on whether you have been sexually harassed and, if so, what you should do. Large organizations also frequently have employee counseling services and program coordinators who you can turn to for advice.[15] Use them! A final source of information and advice is an attorney who is an expert in employment law and who has plenty of experience adjudicating and mediating sexual harassment cases. Just because you consult an outside attorney, however, does not mean that you have to proceed with litigation. You can still follow your organization's grievance procedures, a practice that employers and the EEOC prefer.[16]

Because determining whether a work environment is hostile is more difficult than determining quid pro quo sexual harassment, seeking the opinions of trusted friends and family members *outside* of the work environment can be useful.[17] Outsiders are often more objective than insiders who often know and like the person you might accuse of sexual harassment. However, through discreetly making inquiries on the inside of your organization, you might also learn that you have colleagues who have experienced sexual harassment at the hand of the same person. Teaming with others is particularly smart because a group of victims greatly enhances the credibility of your complaint, provides colleagues to commiserate with, and allows you to share the burden of preparing for any official proceedings.[18] Regardless of whether you address sexual harassment alone or in group, carefully document the date, time, place, and details of the harassing incidents.[19]

If you believe your organization's grievance system has the potential to solve your problem, you are smart to use it. People on the inside will appreciate your not retaining an attorney and taking legal action that typically leads to a more costly, time consuming, and adversarial experience than internal procedures. However, another very common option is to address the problem informally through confronting your alleged perpetrator of harassment.[20] After seeking the advice of one of the expert sources just identified, you can confront the person who you feel has harassed you with the facts of the offensive behavior and with a request to desist from that behavior.

If you want to minimize hard feelings because you have to work with this person, I would initially address him with humility, sincerity, and nonjudgmental sharing of how it makes you feel when the offensive behavior occurs. For example, you can tell the person that you feel objectified, self-conscious, embarrassed, uncomfortable, or unvalued as a woman when he tells you that you look hot, eyes you from head to toe, or gives you an unsolicited backrub. By following this approach, you have not called this person demeaning names (e.g., a shallow, disrespectful, misogynist that he may be) that might exacerbate permanent bad feelings between the two of you. Instead, through giving a man insight into your feelings that he was likely unaware of, he might feel sufficiently sorry to the point of never again behaving in a sexually offensive way. If you take this approach, as well as start with the bad news and end with something good, there is always a chance for a reconciliation that draws you into a more respectful and meaningful relations with the harasser. I sincerely believe that this approach can work with fundamentally good men who, often raised with brothers and a guy's-guy father, really don't know how to treat women but are ever willing to learn. Will this soft approach work with everyone? Heck no. But the potential for and beauty of a solved problem and a reconciled relationship makes this option worthy of consideration.

If the sincere sharing of feelings or the request to desist from offensive behavior fails when you have been perfectly clear about specific behavior you want stopped,[21] my professional recommendation is to warn the perpetrator that, if the hostile behavior continues, you *will* report it to his supervisor or file a grievance. The subsequent step is to report the behavior or to file a grievance as you gradually elevate your actions to more stringent means until the harassment ends. Ultimately, if you are not satisfied with the resolution of your grievance, contemporary organizations often allow you to file an appeal. However, the process does not have to end there. Whenever you feel that justice is not served within your organization, you can pursue representation from the EEOC, your labor union, or your professional organization. Moreover, you can retain an attorney who can represent you in a civil case against the perpetrator and a negligent employer.

Using progressive steps to deal with sexual harassment, however, can be thrown out the window when addressing more egregious infractions such as a superior threatening to fire you for refusing to have sex, or a coworker ripping your clothes off while you resist. Starting by filing a grievance is both acceptable and expected. Not only do you deserve immediate protection, immediate action is needed to help ensure that no one else is subjected to such abuse. When the malevolence of sexual harassment rises to the level of serious threats and actual abuses that compromise a person's livelihood or results in physical harm, the rules of the game change—one strike and you're out becomes the new standard.

Although fear of repercussions may justify a delay in reporting egregious harassment, informing an official of the harassment as soon as possible enhances your credibility, solves the problem sooner, and prevents the awkwardness of explaining why you delayed reporting an incident. Moreover, if you fail to convey an incident to an authority in your organization, you will have a much more difficult time suing your employer because your employer can legitimately claim that it "cannot be held responsible for preventing or correcting harassment that it did not know about."[22] Now, let's take a look at what a follower can do to bring sexual harassment to end.

The Most Effective Practices for Ending Sexual Harassment

The MSPB has conducted the two largest studies addressing victims of sexual harassment. In their study of over 8,500 federal employees reported in 1988, they found that, for both men and women, *asking or telling a person to stop their harassing behavior was the most effective informal way of dealing with unwanted sexual attention.*[23] For women, the second most effective informal approach was threatening to tell others or actually telling others about the sexual harassment. For men, the second most effective approach for dealing with sexual harassment was avoiding the harasser. The study further revealed the following three *formal* actions had the highest percentages of respondents believing that they were very or somewhat effective in helping victims of sexual harassment:

1. Filling a grievance or adverse action appeal
2. Filling a discriminatory complaint
3. Requesting an investigation of my agency

In the MSPB's study of over 8,000 federal employees reported in 1995, asking or telling a person to stop their harassment was, again, the number one informal action perceived to "make things better" for both men and women.[24] Reporting the behavior to a supervisor or other official was the number two ranked informal action that women identified as making things better, whereas for men, threatening to tell or telling others was the number two ranked informal action for making things better.

In addition to assessing the seriousness of a sexual harassment offense, I would like to close by suggesting that you also consider factors that might mitigate the course of action that you chart. As Roy Lubit asserts in *Coping with Toxic Managers, Subordinates . . . and Other Difficult People*, it is emotionally intelligent to determine whether the sexual harassment was committed by someone who is "clueless, depressed and needy, a misogynist, a dinosaur, or someone who feels he has a right

DON'T RISK IT

Several years ago, I cut an article out of the newspaper that told a story about a police officer who was pulling over women because they fit the profile of a fugitive at-large who had a rose tattoo on her breast. To demonstrate mistaken identity, all of the women flashed the cop. I took the article to campus, read it to my students, and laughed at it, not because I thought it was funny, but because it was an act to help illustrate a point relevant to our study of sexual harassment. Fifteen minutes before the class ended, I paused to reveal my true intention and asked everyone to share on a card their anonymous opinion as to whether they thought the story constituted sexual harassment if it wasn't being used for learning purposes. Students shared that the article was no big deal, funny, and certainly not part of a pattern necessary for establishing sexual harassment. Although I agreed that the absence of pattern prevented the behavior from qualifying as sexual harassment, my advice to the class was simple—don't tell entertaining stories or jokes that have sexual overtones. As it turned out, 17 students who registered anonymous opinions did not consider the story to be sexual harassment, but three did. More importantly, all it takes is one person to file a complaint that can cause an enormously time-consuming and emotionally draining legal morass that is likely to result in tarnishing your reputation, even if you are exonerated. More unselfishly, desisting in telling such stories takes a stand against objectifying women or treating them as sex objects instead of colleagues worthy of the same respect that men receive for the talents that they bring to the work environment.

to the entire bounty of his company."[25] A seasoned manager guilty of procuring sex through favors or fear merits more severe consequences than a naïve young yokel who tells his first dirty joke at work. Such discernments are essential for helping you tailor the most effective, fair, and problem-minimizing approach for bringing the sexual harassment to a permanent end. And don't forget, you are never alone—there are many sage sources of support to help you make those discernments.

How to Deal with Abusive, Bullying Bosses

There is nothing worse than going to work every day knowing that you will be psychologically beaten up by an abusive, bullying boss. If you are dealing with a superior who constantly demeans you, is never satisfied, sabotages your work, ruins plans by forcing you to work overtime, or takes pleasure in embarrassing you in front of others, my heart goes out to you. Odds are, you don't deserve it, and a trustworthy plan is needed to help you navigate the landmines that you tiptoe around on a daily basis.

Much of what has been already said about how to deal with micromanagers and bosses who give you unethical assignments also applies to the abusive boss. Let's touch on where overlapping approaches exist and then turn our attention to the unique measures that are needed in dealing with abusive, bullying bosses. The three leading overlapping recommendations are:

1. Find another job.
2. Carefully document the abusive behavior.
3. Approach the boss or the boss's superior with a group of people who share a concern over the bad behavior.

I realize that finding another job may cause you to feel like a quitter or failure; however, every psychologist, psychiatrist, or counselor I have ever known will tell you that you have more control over your own behavior than someone else's. Finding another job puts you in control for a change. In contrast to feeling like a quitter, you should pat yourself on the back for pursuing a career that includes people who respect and care about you. Unfortunately, finding another job doesn't satisfy the short-run need to deal with an abusive boss. So, what do you do? Let's focus on new twists on old approaches, as well as approaches that have not already been addressed.

New Wrinkles on Enhancing the Boss's Self-Worth and Making Yourself Indispensable

I will never forget being asked by a new colleague if my wife and I would like to get season tickets together for UA's home football games. I found the colleague to be arrogant and a chronic complainer and wasn't sure that I wanted to sit with him through an entire football season. Not having the heart to say no, I consented and was very surprised by what evolved. A friendship developed over the football season and so did a special collegial relationship at work. Ultimately, this person turned out to be the most loyal, supportive, thoughtful, reliable, and sensitive colleague in my department. This experience inadvertently reinforced the importance of a simple discernment that I encourage my students to make before choosing a path for dealing with difficult people:

Are you dealing with a spoiled child or a neglected child?

If you are parents, then you know that dealing with spoiled children and dealing with neglected children require quite different strategies. In retrospect, I believe that my seemingly arrogant, chronically complaining colleague was a neglected child who simply needed a little attention, which occurred through sitting together through a football season.

This experience also causes me to appreciate a counterintuitive strategy advocated by Dr. Gini Scott, author of *A Survival Guide to Bad Bosses*, for dealing with a new boss who is showing abusive tendencies.[26] Knowing that a new boss is experiencing the burden of moving and adjusting, as well as likely experiencing some loneliness, she recommends throwing a party for him and other acts of kindness to make your supervisor feel liked and welcomed. The probability of this approach having a positive result is high enough to merit the effort and cost, and if the strategy doesn't work, you can take comfort knowing that you've likely done nothing that will make the situation worse.

To make yourself indispensable to the boss, Gonzague Dufour, author of *Managing Your Manager: How to Get Ahead with Any Type of Boss*, recommends that you perform tasks that the abusive boss hates or is not good at.[27] For example, insightful bosses who are inclined to bully often know that they do not have the skills for handling people-related problems. If you are fortunate to have better people skills and can relieve the boss of dealing with people problems, then you increase your value to the boss, which often results in better treatment.

Approaches Unique to Addressing Abusive Bosses

Control Your Behavior and Hold Your Ground

When an abusive, bullying boss is trying to destroy your ideas with a nasty, demeaning tirade, it is perfectly natural to become overwhelmed with anger and to display behavior ranging from mild uneasiness to completely falling apart. Feel all the emotions you want, but don't display them. Unlike normal people who are inclined to back off when they see your pain, bullies are ruthless and do just the opposite. As Lubit aptly notes, "Sharks go after wounded swimmers. . . . Don't let them know you are hurting."[28] Through standing tall on issues and refusing to show any weakness or emotions when attacked, you deny the bully the reaction that he or she desires.[29] Typically, bullies will consequently back off to refocus their torment on those who are more inclined to give them the cowering reaction that they covet.

Don't Be a Yes-Man or Woman

Although complying with everything an abusive boss wants may seem to be the wisest way to prevent abuse, Dufour claims this is a "huge mistake."[30] Bullies are pragmatists who, above all, want followers who can help them achieve their goals. While they may not like being challenged, they will appreciate counsel that brings them desired results. Dufour, however, advises you to be judicious in challenging the boss—pick your battles carefully in order to avoid losing your job.[31] Because bullies are impatient, he also encourages you to address them with a concise, well-rehearsed logic that emphasizes the positive outcome of your ideas.

Confront the Boss and Stay Away

Yes, the experts instruct you to do both. Gini Scott encourages employees not to put up with verbal abuse from superiors.[32] Her advice is to schedule a meeting with the boss as soon as possible to explain calmly why rude remarks were inappropriate and to ask the boss how you can improve your work. Lubit concurs, but he foregoes the idea of labeling the boss as rude or any other pejorative.[33] Instead, his instructions are to (1) clarify that certain language or behavior is affecting your motivation and performance and (2) suggest alternative approaches that allow you to deliver peak performances. A pathological and dim-witted boss might continue the abusive behavior, but others will wisely choose to treat you in a way that will optimize your performance and thus make them look good.

Amy Smith and Roy Lubit also encourage avoiding abusive bosses, especially when you can predict their foul moods, in order to limit their opportunities to chip away at your psychological well-being.[34] Setting aside time to vent emotions and develop a thoughtful strategy for dealing with an abusive boss is a necessity. However, placing limits on the amount of time you spend thinking about the boss's bad behavior is also a necessity to prevent unhealthy obsessing or a prolonged, unproductive fixation on the boss. Remember, it is unlikely that you are the cause of the abusive behavior, so you cannot take the boss's bad conduct personally. The abusive boss has not earned the right to hold your time and emotions hostage both day and night.

Experts argue that avoidance causes other performance problems symptomatic of not addressing the source of work stress.[35] While I am attracted to the idea of addressing the causes of problems rather than avoiding problems, I think that it is essential to discern whether you or you with your peers have a reasonable chance of bringing about change in an abusive boss. I do not recommend *overtly* taking on a smart, highly motivated, pathological supervisor when your job security is at stake or you do not have a backdoor to another job. Avoidance to ensure survival is the wise move when there is a distinct possibility of losing in a showdown. When you know that you are outmatched, however, you still have numerous options: the confrontation approaches in table 10.1 that maintain your anonymity.

At the most general level, my recommendation for dealing with abusive bosses concurs with Roy Lubit's: "Above all, do what is needed to maintain your sanity, self-esteem, and health."[36] However, if you are mentally and physically in sound shape, consider confronting abusive bosses as a moral obligation to protect future innocent employees from the wrath of the abuser. But never forget to confront in a manner that also protects you from that wrath!

CHAPTER 12

Summary and Stories of Follower Glories

As a professor, I used to be surprised by students who can memorize every detail of their lecture notes in preparation for an examination yet remain totally clueless as to the overriding message and principle of a lecture. However, when I paused to do what I instruct students to do, which is to look first in the mirror for the causes of problems, I realized that I was largely to blame for the rote memorization and that the solution was really quite simple. I could tell my students the overriding message, or, better yet, I could design an exercise where the students derive the message themselves. Since the former format is more realistic for this book, what follows is a summary of the major message from each chapter. If you have the time, however, see if you can derive a one- or two-sentence overriding message for each chapter, and then compare your messages to mine.

Summary Messages: Secrets to Success in Supporting Roles

Chapter 1: *Don't be seduced by leadership roles.* Leadership is a romanticized, overrated role that, for many, is destined to disappoint through excessive demands and a limited capacity to impact organizational performance.

Chapter 2: *You do not need to be the official leader to have a substantial impact on organizations and individuals.* Followers can be informal leaders without the formal trappings and demands of formal leadership positions.

Chapter 3: *To become an ideal follower, strive to be more active than passive and develop your communication and interpersonal skills.*

Chapter 4: *Identify triggers for old habits, and substitute new follower skills when old habits are triggered.* Reinforce new follower skills through structures and especially support from family and friends.

Chapter 5: *Discern your unique followership style.* Determine whether you are active versus passive, conforming versus individualistic, committed versus alienated, pragmatic versus idealistic, and self-serving versus altruistic.

Chapters 6 and 7: *Pursue employment and membership in organizations that are compatible with your followership style.* Your followership style should be compatible with your organization's climate, culture, and leadership styles.

Chapter 8: *Seek employment in organizations where jobs are well designed, employees are treated fairly, and management behaves with integrity.* Steer clear of organizational politics, ambiguous and conflicting roles, and organizations that breach their contracts with employees.

Chapter 9: *Investigate and consider working in follower jobs that are consistently ranked highly.* Consider employment in engineering jobs as well as jobs in healthcare, the financial sector, and the computer industry. Do not be seduced by jobs such as actor, police officer, photojournalist, broadcaster, and firefighter.

Chapters 10 and 11: *Develop the follower skills to deal effectively with micromanagers, unethical supervisors, sexual harassers, and abusive bosses.*

Two Overriding Messages

Finally, although the preceding major messages are my best generalizations based on research, don't forget another significant lesson—you may be the exception to any of the messages in this book. You may love executive leadership roles, monotonous jobs may not bother you, or a career in photojournalism may be your perfect fit. However, the most significant overall message from this book is this:

> Being the ideal follower from the perspective of management is only part of winning at following. You win at following through working in jobs that bring you satisfaction in organizations that are compatible with your natural followership style. Put simply, to win at following, become an invaluable subordinate working in jobs that you love in organizations that love you back.

Let's turn to some stories that reinforce the major message from chapter 2.

Followers Who Lead

Loud, rowdy, and chaotic—these are three words that best describe what it's like to share a meal with my wife's Lebanese family. It's an Americanization of a Middle-Eastern happening that all WASPs need to experience to expand their sense of humor and revel in what it means to live to eat and celebrate.

Mixed in with my wife's family are various in-laws of Western European descent who are a bit more reserved. When around 60 family members gather for a Thanksgiving or Easter celebration, arguably the quietest and most reserved family member is my nephew, Mike Bobo, that is, until you put a football uniform on him. Mike is a natural athlete with a tenacious desire to win and a superb mentor in his father who coached professional football for the New York Giants. The convergence of these forces destined Mike to be a star, as he won the 1993 High School Player of the Year in the state of Georgia as the quarterback of the Thomasville High School football team.[1] Signing to play for The University of Georgia, Mike continued on his star trajectory as he lettered his freshman year and won the starting quarterback job as a sophomore. By the fourth game of his second season, Mike was one of the leading quarterbacks in the SEC as he completed 60.7 percent of his passes and had a quarterback rating of 151.9.[2] Tragically, in the second quarter of the fourth game of the season against Ole Miss, Mike's promising year came to an end as he took a bone-breaking hit to his left knee that sidelined him for the rest of the season. Meanwhile, UGA's season culminated with a six and six win-loss record and the firing of head coach, Ray Goff.

Mike rehabbed, returned to the team for spring practice, and regained his starting role as the quarterback for the 1996 season. Playing under UGA's new coach, Jim Donnan, the Bulldogs won 5 of 11 games, including only 3 of 8 games in the SEC. Mike completed only 50.9 percent of his passes, and his efficiency rating slipped to a dismal 113.6.[3] Although Bulldog fans wanted to give Jim Donnan a chance, they were also in shock and scared to death that the Donnan era was going to fare worse than the Ray Goff era when the Bulldogs went 0–5 against Tennessee, 1–6 against Florida, and 2–4–1 against Auburn. The most concerned fan and athlete was Georgia's quarterback, Mike Bobo.

Many athletes can accept a loss knowing that they practiced and played their hearts out. Mike is not one of them. If you lose, it is because you didn't work hard enough or figure out how to win. Moreover, when you have teammates such as Hines Ward and Robert Edwards, there is no excuse for losing.[4] Determined to turn around the team, seniors

Mike, Hines, and Robert decided to rally the team with the goal of play-ing in a New Year's Day bowl game and earning a ranking among the top 10 teams in the country.[5] Resolved also to set a sterling example for the underclassmen, and one in particular by the name of Champ Bailey, Mike hit the weight room with a vengeance, lost 18 pounds, and started his senior season in the best shape of his life.[6] Most importantly, Mike, Hines, and Robert literally assumed the role of coaches in conducting off-season conditioning and practices from January until the start of spring practice and from the end of spring practice through July. In essence, Mike, Hines and Robert, followers of Coach Donnan and his assistant coaches, became the informal leaders of the team in the off-season.

Well, what happened in the 1997 season? The Bulldogs went 10 and 2, beat the Wisconsin Badgers by a score of 33 to 6 in the Outback Bowl, and finished the season ranked 10th in the nation by the Asso-ciated Press. Unfortunately, the Bulldogs were unable to win the SEC, as Peyton Manning led the University of Tennessee to that honor. Few know, though, that Peyton Manning, the NFL's number one draft choice in 1998 and arguably the most prolific quarterback in NFL history, was not the statistically top-rated quarterback in the SEC his senior year—Mike Bobo was.[7]

But this last point is simply bragging about my nephew. My major point is to reinforce the message of chapter 2: *You do not need to be the official leader to have a substantial impact on organizations and individuals.*

Inspirational Followers: Leadership without Trying

Mike Bobo conscientiously assumed an informal leadership role on his 1997 football team. He was an athlete with rare physical talent, but more relevant to this book, he was a follower with a rare drive to suc-ceed that pushed him to act conscientiously as an informal leader in order to affect an entire athletic team.

By contrast, in *Followership*, a must read, Harvard lecturer Barbara Kellerman tells stories of followers working together to bring about broad organizational, institutional, and cultural change.[8] However, in this chapter, I would like to focus on individual followers, such as you, who deeply affect the lives of others, even though they might not exer-cise formal *or* informal initiatives to act as a leader. When I think of the individuals who have inspired my life, none of them were formal leaders at the time, none of them had the notoriety of a star athlete or coach, and none of them had any idea of their profound influence on me.

A German, Two Mexicans, and a Native American

Although this might sound as though I am setting you up for some kind of racial or xenophobic joke, a German, two Mexicans, and a Native American were actually members of a team that I worked with one summer between my sophomore and junior years in college. Paid poorly for our positions, we were primarily pickle packers paired up to push pickles into pint-sized jars. (How is that for alliteration?) Seriously, our job was to move pickles from enormous vats to progressively smaller containers with our worst days being spent shoving pickles into the small jars that ended up on the shelves of grocery stores. The work was monotonous and physically exhausting. We labored from 7:30 a.m. until 3:30 p.m. with two 10-minute breaks and a half-hour for lunch. By the end of the workday, my fingernails were stained green, and my pants were so starched with gunk that they could almost stand vertically on their own. I could not wait to jettison the job. After a month and one-half, I was relieved to land a job as a roofer—one of the 20 worst jobs in America according to CareerCast (see table 9.7 in chapter 9), but not nearly as oppressive as working in the pickle factory.

Now, what was so profound and inspirational about working with this group of followers? For one, despite the poor pay and distasteful work, my coworkers had terrific work ethics that set an example for me that has lasted a lifetime. I learned that if you accept a job, the honorable behavior is to do the job, regardless of the pay and nature of the work. Second, although I was, ironically, a minority in this group, I was accepted and treated with respect by my coworkers. By contrast, I realized that if the roles were reversed, it would be highly unlikely that my homogeneous peer group in college would be nearly as accepting. Mexican Americans and Native Americans were not part of the sisterhood of Chi Omega or Tri Delta or the brotherhood of SAE or Sigma Chi on my campus. Yet my coworkers were inadvertently destroying every preconceived notion and stereotype that prevented them from gaining membership in these elitist collegiate social organizations. Moreover, I began learning that, despite my chauvinism for my own culture, the egalitarian values of many Native American cultures and the significance of family in Hispanic culture were fascinating, admirable, and worthy of lionization rather than derogation.

Finally, I could not make sense of the contrast between my status in life versus theirs. I was working this summer job to make chump change to help pay for bar bills and frat parties when I returned to college in the fall. By contrast, the pickle factory was their full-time job. Moreover, not only did my coworkers labor at this awful job from 7:30 to 3:30, more than one returned home, ate dinner, and headed out to second jobs as janitors in office parks and school buildings. Why were the shoes not reversed? Why did I enjoy the easier life? Having no knowledge of how they were changing my life, a German, two Mexicans, a Native American—the lowest-level followers on the floor of a nasty pickle factory—had sown the seeds that would eventually define my values and character as an adult.

Although the seeds were planted, I have to admit that, at age 20, I still needed some fertilization and irrigation. My garden was not going to bloom much beyond chickweed, dandelions, and crabgrass without the skilled care of a master gardener and some maintenance workers. Those key players in my life are Joe, Gillie, Susan, and Matthew—four unsuspecting followers who are all likely confused and amused to think that someone would consider them inspirational leaders.

Joe, the Master Gardener

When I was 11 years old, we packed our bags and headed across the Ohio River to a world that was quite different from what we had grown accustomed to in Ohio. My father had accepted a job at the University of Kentucky in Lexington. Whether the differences were culturally based or simply reflecting the throes of pubescence and junior high school, I will never know. However, I do know that a lot of people spoke with an accent that enthralled and amused me in Kentucky and that the security in the similarity of the people in the suburbs of Columbus, Ohio, had vanished. Lexington was a city of wealth and poverty—a city small enough that the public schools could not avoid mixing the children from both backgrounds. There were the country club kids who snubbed you and the kids from more humble backgrounds who scared you with their thuggish ways or unkempt appearances. An oasis in the middle of the madness was a neighborhood kid by the name of Joe.

On the surface, Joe and I had nothing in common. Peaking at six feet five inches, Joe was the tallest kid in his class. I was aptly described by my father as the world's largest midget. Joe played the flute and piccolo in the band, while I played a different sport every season. While Joe had rich, thick, dark brown hair in a fashionably hip style for the Beatlemania era of hair in the early to mid-1960s, no one knew what my hair really looked like because it was always cut to a quarter-inch length for the Cro-Magnon coaches who thought long hair was for sissies. The short hair, in turn, was ideal for emphasizing the dimensions of my face and a complexion that made for a class picture that was perfect for a game of connect the dots. Joe, in turn, escaped puberty with a complexion that never bore a blemish. Ultimately, while Joe was getting to first and second base in parlor games, the best I could do was to round a base or two on a baseball diamond.

Ironically, although Joe had more going for him than I did, he was painfully shy around school and among kids who were not part of our neighborhood's inner circle. Handsome, smart, and wise beyond his age, he still perceived himself to be a mutant giant, the klutzy son of a college football player, and the dumb little brother of a Phi Beta Kappa at Duke University. Dragging him to a school dance or teen nightclub was like pulling teeth, and when he broke down and attended, he was often a six-foot-five wallflower. Yet among his friends, he was witty, clever, and full of personality. He had *Playboy* magazines hidden in cinder blocks in his basement, gave all his friends nicknames, had the latest Beatles albums, called his mother "Ruby-baby" (to her face!), and discretely shared his adventures with the bases that I had not yet encountered with the opposite sex. Unable to share a friendship through sports, the school band, or any extracurricular activities, we found a common bond in our need for pranks, experimentation, and testing people's patience. We smoked cigars in the woods, purposefully drove into the country and got lost on a double date, and egged and toilet papered houses. One of our favorite pranks was to stuff me inside his hide-a-bed couch with nothing more than my hand eerily exposed on the seat cushion.

Joe's pranks were never cruel or destructive, just imaginative and fun. Yet my bond with Joe that has lasted a lifetime is much more than the good times. While I was an awkward and naïve teen with a bottomless pit of insecurities, Joe was always a listening ear, a chorus of confidence boosting, and bastion of insight and wisdom shared with an empathy and concern that was as palpable as his six-foot-five looming presence.

Strangely, the leadership influence of Joe the follower did not really materialize until I was in my late 30s. In a random call simply to catch up with Joe, my lifelong best friend abruptly blurted out something that had nothing to do with our conversation or anything that we had ever talked about in our 28-year friendship. The fact that it was so irrelevant to the conversation accentuated that he was telling me something that was eating away at him that he could not hold back any longer. Joe announced that he was gay. So, what does this have to do with Joe being a de facto inspirational leader in his followership roles in life?

Like my pickle-packing coworkers, Joe obliterated preconceived notions and stereotypes. At the time of my phone call, Joe was living in New York City after a stint working for the Federal Maritime

Commission in DC. When I asked him when he came out of the closet, he shared that it was while he was working in DC. This was a surprise to me because when I last visited him in New York City, we necessarily crashed in the same queen-size bed in his tiny efficiency apartment. Without thinking, I blurted, "But Joe, we shared the same bed the last time I visited you in New York." Joe, in turn, with a kindness that I did not deserve, calmly proceeded to bury the stereotype of gay men with uncontrollable sex drives living a life of debauchery. He replied, "Norm, I know that you are heterosexual, and I would never disrespect that." Stupid me for making such a comment. Of course, he would not disrespect my sexual preference; his track record indicated that he *had* respected my heterosexuality for nearly three decades of friendship.

But Joe's influence on my life is much more than teaching me a lesson about stereotyping. Having a best friend who is one of the most principled and caring persons that I have ever known, I want Joe to have every right, privilege, and respect that every citizen of this country enjoys. While a German, two Mexicans, and a Native American had planted seeds, Joe cultivated the seeds without ever making a single political statement. All he did was be a terrific best friend. In turn, I became a minority rights activist.

I have experienced many more losing than winning battles in fighting for Joe's rights as well as fighting for causes that would further dignify racial minorities in the Deep South. As you well know by now, I come from a family full of jocks, and we all hate to lose—at anything! However, I also have been blessed to have three very special people in my life. Many would say they are followers, but to me, they are inspirational leaders who remind me that life is good and that anything can be done with know-how and determination. Let me now tell you about Gillie, Susan, and Matthew—the trio that maintains my spirits and keeps me fighting for causes that Joe and my pickle-packing coworkers inspired.

Gillie, Susan, and Matthew

I group this dynamic trio together because they share three things in common—a compassionate, charitable heart; relentless determination; and a happiness that is infectious. Gillie is a special education teacher in an elementary school in Tuscaloosa, Alabama, where she has dedicated 39 years of her life to helping children with learning disabilities develop remedial reading, math, and writing skills. [9] The job, however, is much more than that. Gillie has the challenging task of teaching students with attention deficit disorder, autism, and hyperactivity problems how to function effectively in society through managing their anger and frustrations. Any special education teacher would contend that the work is demanding, but for Gillie, those demands are magnified because she insists that her students exceed the standards of her school district and profession. To that end, her work necessitates a listening ear, an open mind, and a flexible approach to teaching. Yet the single most vital human characteristic required for her work is patience, which she says is only sustainable with a bulletproof ego and a sense of humor, two qualities that she possesses in spades. Beyond her devotion to special needs children, Gillie serves her community through a small Presbyterian congregation that provides food for 750 people in need each month and is the first church to speak out against violations of the civil liberties of various minority groups. I got to know Gillie through yet another cause that she supports—Alabama Arise, an interest group that advocates for low-income citizens of Alabama. As part of a team put together by Alabama Arise, Gillie and I lobbied the state legislature where I had the privilege of observing firsthand the brilliance of her artistry in advocating for the underprivileged.

Gillie demonstrated a talent for laying out the cold, hard, ugly facts of injustice in the context of broader conversations and interactions that include lots of laughter and taking delight in our state senators and representatives. Beyond getting her political message across, she simultaneously conveyed two additional messages: "I like you, and I'm having a good time hanging out with you." With her happy-dog attitude toward life, capacity to find humor in everything, and laughter that makes others feel as if they are stand-up comics, Gillie is a follower leading a lot of people around with her inspiring causes, magnetic personality, and a sense that good times have arrived whenever she enters a room. While Gillie is the quintessential role model for how to humor people into submission, she is, more importantly, a sterling example of how to hate the sin but love the sinner.

Susan, in turn, is a medical and psychiatric therapist with a teenage energy and joy for life that belies her age.[10] While I have no idea if her red hair is a function of her DNA or Clairol, I *do* know that it is the perfect symbol of her extroverted personality and spunk. Born and raised in the country just outside of Montgomery, Alabama, Susan is a Southern belle who loves being made a fuss over by Southern gentlemen. Yet her basic nature is to make an even bigger fuss over her family, friends, Southern beaus, and patients. She is plainly and simply a giver who operates at a pace rivaling the Energizer Bunny's.

An employee of the Veterans Administration most of her career, Susan has embraced the challenges of working with military personnel struggling with pathologies ranging from post-traumatic stress syndrome and depression to schizophrenia and bipolar disorder. Her drive for successful therapy has demanded an ocean of empathy and acceptance as well as assiduous and continuous training to master the most contemporary knowledge and skills necessary for the enormous intellectual and emotional demands of her job. As she has aptly noted, when you are working with suicidal patients, there is no room for error or lapses in effort or emotional commitment.

Caring about the physical and emotional pain of others is a wonderful virtue to possess or cultivate. Being concerned about others enough to develop the knowledge and skills to comfort and heal those who suffer elevates care to a higher level of virtue. However, the most virtuous level of care is reflected in the behavior of Susan. Beyond caring and caring enough about others to equip herself with the knowledge and skills to minister to them, she has the fortitude to *persist* in her provision of care when others fall by the wayside due to physical or emotional exhaustion. Susan's care for people who struggle with mental health combines empathy with the knowledge of and fortitude for healing. I believe that the quality of care provided by Susan as a follower is unmistakably a leadership example of our culture's most extoled virtue—love.

My great-nephew, Matthew, is the final character in the triad of people I admire for their joyful, unselfish, and persevering examples.[11] To visualize Matthew is to imagine a relatively big, good-looking 21-year-old with military-length dark brown hair, classic facial features with a hint of his grandmother's Lebanese genes, and, most notably, the type of smile that could turn a funeral into a party. However, beware of the smile—it is often a gloat from getting your goat with some kind of prank. Matthew is quite simply a charismatic young man who has that "it" factor that causes people to like him within moments of meeting him.

While popular kids like Matthew often have little more than good looks, perhaps a sense of humor, and a warm hello and goodbye, Matthew began surprising people with his generosity and concern for underdogs at a very young age. In the third grade, he won $128 by correctly guessing the amount of money in a Coke bottle at a Youth Service Connection carnival in Athens, Georgia. He boasted to his buddies that he was going to use the money to buy PlayStation games. However, on his way home from the carnival, his family slipped into a Saturday evening mass, and Matthew, with unflappable resolve, gave all of his winnings

COURAGE AND ACCOMPLISHMENT WITH A SUPPORTING CAST

As a vivacious seven-year-old about to begin the second grade, Susan was stricken with polio. With the disease attacking the neurons in her spinal cord, she became completely paralyzed from the neck down, except for the capacity to wiggle some toes on her right foot and some fingers on her right hand. To restore some functionality in her legs, Susan underwent 17 corrective surgeries between the ages of 7 and 17 but was never able to regain the ability to walk independently. Confined to a wheelchair, Susan managed to complete elementary school, junior and senior high school, an undergraduate degree, and a master of social work degree *prior* to public facilities becoming handicapped accessible. Her schools had no elevators, no bathroom stalls to accommodate wheelchairs, and no handicapped parking.

While receiving treatment at the Roosevelt Warm Springs Institute for Rehabilitation in Georgia, Susan completed the second grade in two months with the help of tutors. To complete the third and fourth grades, her first-grade teacher brought her schoolwork to Susan's home and tutored her. Fortunately for Susan, her elementary and junior high schools were one story, but to attend classes at Sidney Lanier High School in Montgomery, her brother Paul had to pull her wheelchair up the stairs of the three-story school house. To attend her classes in college, two or three brothers from Acacia fraternity, in turn, would carry Susan up and down the stairwells of the multistory buildings on the campus of The University of Alabama.

Susan's educational achievements reflect her fearless determination and the support from a small cast of characters to whom she gives all of the credit. However, I am constantly amazed that she holds nothing back from enjoying *all* possible aspects of life. As my friend who is most likely to throw a party or have a house full of dinner guests, there is no doubt that Susan will go to her deathbed having lived a more active and complete life than 99 percent of the people who are blessed to stand on two healthy legs their entire lives.

to Father Jack to help build a nursing facility to care for poor people without health insurance.

Matthew's penchant for generating money for everyone but himself is the hallmark of his youthful life. Each year, he raises $6,000 for a charity called Extra Special People (ESP) that provides programs and training to empower children with developmental disabilities.[12] Through one of ESP's events called Jump Fly, people pay Matthew to participate in skydiving exhibitions, and, in turn, he donates all of the money to ESP.

In recent years, Matthew became a mentor to an elementary school student who has a learning disability and a difficult home life. He then decided to hone his public speaking skills and now travels to elementary schools throughout Georgia to give free motivational speeches to children about timely topics such as bullying, accepting people who are different, and overcoming life's challenges. His presentations to children have been so relevant, effective, and entertaining that he is now in demand for adult audiences, as he has become a featured speaker at conventions and conferences for school administrators. While teens and young adults are typically preoccupied with self, Matthew cannot seem to give away enough money, sage advice, and huge smiles to everyone who comes into his life. I am unaware of Matthew ever being a formal leader of a club, class, or organization, but to me, he is the leading example of generosity and unselfishness in our family. In my most downtrodden moments, he is also a faith-restoring reminder that someone pure in heart is among us.

Closing Observation and Thought

In concluding my discussion about Gillie, Susan, and Matthew, I would like to share one last commonality that allows these dynamic individuals to be inspirational leaders disguised as followers. Gillie loves to go to movies, but she only hears the soundtrack because congenital cataracts, detached retinas, and eye infections from botched surgeries have left her blind. Susan loves to dance and continues to attend dances, but she has not danced on her feet in 60 years because she was crippled by polio and confined to a wheelchair at the age of 7. Finally, Matthew still loves to skydive, but he no longer jumps out of airplanes because he suffers from cerebral palsy, which led to a collapsed lung in recent years. Restricted to a wheelchair, he has never been able to play team sports, dance, or drive a car. Just as dancing was taken away from Susan, the only sport that Matthew could participate in—tandem sky diving—has been taken away from him.

AN INDOMITABLE SPIRIT

In her 29th week of pregnancy, my niece, Suzanne, began to experience strange abdominal pains causing her to think that she was going into labor. Rushed to the hospital, she soon learned that her uterus had ruptured and that she must give premature birth to the child that she was carrying—Matthew. Requiring four blood transfusions in his first week of life and under constant watch in a neonatal intensive care unit for seven weeks, Matthew's chance of surviving infancy was uncertain. But a fighter from the beginning, the three-and-one-half-pound Matthew rallied to hang on to life. Whether he would ever walk, talk, attend school, and experience any quality of life were highly questionable and, ultimately, the great unknown.

Under the knife for at least 10 surgeries and experiencing a life of constant therapy, Matthew has made substantial physical progress but has never been able to sustain the capacity to walk on his own. However, his intellectual development and achievements have surpassed all expectations. Entering high school with fifth-grade mathematic skills, numerous administrators and teachers wrote Matthew off as a lost cause incapable of graduating from high school. Boy, did they underestimate his aptitude and, especially, his relentless determination. By the end of his first year of high school, Matthew had jumped four levels to master ninth-grade math. By the end of four years of high school, Matthew not only graduated on time with the rest of his class, he sported a 3.5 grade point average.

All three of these individuals greet each morning having to overcome enormous obstacles that you and I will likely never have to address. Yet, they begin each day with a joyful spirit, courageous resolve, and a commitment to the needs of others that they put before the daunting needs of their own. I am fortunate to be born into a unique family full of "jocks and docs" who have modeled a wonderful standard of aspiration for the gridiron, classroom, and occupations. However, the biggest influences in my life are a team of pickle packers, a gay best friend, a nephew and a social worker confined to wheelchairs, and a blind elementary school teacher who is likely somewhere at this moment celebrating the day and laughing away in the middle of doing a good deed. To many, these people are simple followers, but to me, they are much more than followers and, for that matter, much more than leaders. They are individuals who amaze me and inspire my life—paragons of hope and virtue and the heroes to whom I dedicate this book.

Notes

Preface

1. EBSCO Discovery Service, accessed January 19, 2015.
2. Lydia Saad, "The '40-Hour' Workweek Is Actually Longer—by Seven Hours," accessed January 19, 2015, http://www.gallup.com/poll/175286/hour-workweek-actually-longer-seven-hours.aspx.
3. Lawrence J. Peter and Raymond Hull, *The Peter Principle: Why Good Things Always Go Wrong* (New York: William Morrow, 1969).

Chapter 1

1. U.S. Department of Education, National Center for Education Statistics, "Fast Facts: Teacher Trends," accessed November 30, 2016, nces.ed.gov/fastfacts/display.asp?id=28.
2. ABI Inform, accessed January 27, 2015.
3. Publications refers to books, journal articles, dissertations, theses, magazines, conference papers and proceedings, reports, wire feeds, working papers, newspapers, and audio and video works.
4. EBSCO Discovery Services, accessed January 27, 2015.
5. U.S. Library of Congress, accessed Jan 27, 2015, http://www.loc.gov/.
6. Judith M. Brown, *Gandhi: Prisoner of Hope* (New Haven: Yale University Press, 1990).
7. Ken Burns, *The Roosevelts: An Intimate History*, PBS broadcast September 14, 2014.
8. Nelson Mandela, *Long Walk to Freedom. The Autobiography of Nelson Mandela* (Boston: Little Brown, 1994).

9. BBC News, "Cameron Reveals Big Speech Secret," last updated December 20, 2007, http://news.bbc.co.uk/2/hi/uk_news/politics/7153654 .stm; Walter Isaacson, *Steve Jobs* (New York: Simon & Schuster, 2011).

10. Susan D. Baker, "Followership: The Theoretical Foundation of a Contemporary Construct." *Journal of Leadership and Organizational Studies* 14, no. 1 (2007): 55; James R. Meindl, Standford B. Ehrlich, and Janet M. Dukerich, "The Romanticism of Leadership." *Administrative Science Quarterly* 30, no. 1 (1985): 78–102.

11. Susan D. Baker, "Followership: The Theoretical Foundation of a Contemporary Construct." *Journal of Leadership and Organizational Studies* 14, no. 1 (2007): 55; James R. Meindl et al., "The Romanticism of Leadership."

12. James Rosenau, "Followership and Discretion: Assessing the Dynamics of Modern Leadership," *Harvard International Review* 26, no. 3 (2004): 17.

13. Robert E. Kelley, *The Power of Followership* (New York: Doubleday Currency, 1992), 7–8.

14. *LSU Miracle Victory over Tennessee 16–14*, accessed November 1, 2014. http://www.youtube.com/watch?v=7mAHgD-8k9U.

15. Forbes, "The Most Valuable NFL Teams," accessed August 6, 2016, http://www.forbes.com/pictures/mlm45efhhk/1-dallas-cowboys-2 /#2475563854f5.

16. Tennessee Athletics, *2012 Tennessee Football Roster*, accessed August 6, 2016, http://www.utsports.com/sports/m-footbl/archive/tenn-m -footbl-mtt-2012.html.

17. Derek V. Dooley, in discussion with the author, July 2016.

18. Financial Times, "Executive MBA Ranking 2015," *Financial Times,* accessed August 23, 2016, http://rankings.ft.com/businessschool rankings/executive-mba-ranking-2015.

19. Anderson School of Management, University of California Los Angeles, "Curriculum," accessed September 10, 2014, http://www.anderson .ucla.edu/degrees/mba-program/curriculum.

20. Booth School of Business, University of Chicago, "Executive MBA Curriculum," accessed September 10, 2014, http://www.chicagobooth .edu/programs/exec-mba/academics/curriculum.

21. Fuqua School of Management, Duke University, "Curriculum," accessed September 10, 2014, http://www.tuqua.duke.edu/programs /duke_mba/weekend_executive/curriculum/.

22. Kellogg School of Management, Northwestern University, "Kellogg Executive MBA Program Core Courses," accessed September 9, 2014,

http://www.kellogg.northwestern.edu/programs/emba/courses_curriculum/core_courses.aspx.

23. Wharton School of Business, University of Pennsylvania, "Executive MBA Program Curriculum Overview," accessed September 9, 2014, http://www.wharton.upenn.edu/mbaexecutive/academics/curriculum.

24. Daniel F. Tortora, *The Right Dog for You* (New York: Simon and Schuster, 1980).

25. Chris Whipple and Stephen Stept, *The President's Gatekeepers*, Discovery Channel, broadcast September 11–12, 2013.

Chapter 2

1. Steven F. Hipple, "Self-Employment in the United States," *Monthly Labor Review* (September 2010): 17.

2. Joseph Rost, "Followership, an Outmoded Concept," in *The Art of Followership*, ed. Ronald E. Riggio, Ira Chaleff, and Jean Lipman-Blumen (San Francisco: Jossey-Bass, 2008), 61.

3. Robert E. Kelley, *The Power of Followership* (New York: Doubleday Currency, 1992), 29.

4. Lawrence J. Peter and Raymond Hull, *The Peter Principle: Why Good Things Always Go Wrong* (New York: William Morrow, 1969).

5. Jean E. Smith, *Grant* (New York: Simon & Schuster, 2001).

6. The National World War II Museum, "By the Numbers: World-Wide Deaths," accessed October 20, 2015, http://www.nationalww2museum.org/learn/education/for-students/ww2-history/ww2-by-the-numbers/world-wide-deaths.html.

7. U.S. Department of Labor, Bureau of Labor Statistics Economic, "News Release," accessed October 9, 2014; John Zappe, "Survey Says Executive Tenure Shortening," *ExecuNet*, accessed October 9, 2014, http://www.ere.net/2009/05/28/survey-says-executive-tenure-shortening/.

8. John K. Butler Jr., "A Global View of Informal Organization," *Advanced Management Journal*, 51, no. 3 (1986): 39.

9. Chester I. Barnard, *The Functions of the Executive* (Cambridge, MA: Harvard University, 1938).

10. Tiziana Casciaro and Miguel S. Lobo, "When Competence Is Irrelevant: The Role of Interpersonal Affect in Task-related Ties." *Administrative Science Quarterly* 53 (2008): 655–684; Liangfu Wu and Bruce Rocheleau, "Formal versus Informal End User Training in Public and Private Sector Organizations," *Public Performance and Management Review* 24, no. 4 (2001): 312–321.

11. John R. P. French Jr. and Bertram H. Raven, "The Bases of Social Power," in *Studies in Social Power,* ed. Dorwin Cartwright (Ann Arbor, MI: Institute for Social Research, 1959), 150–167.

12. Chris Argyris, *Integrating the Individual and the Organization* (Piscataway, NJ: Transaction Publisher, 1964).

13. Loren Falkenberg and Irene Herremans, "Ethical Behaviours in Organizations: Directed by the Formal or Informal Systems?" *Journal of Business Ethics* 14 (1995): 133–143; Kathy Williams, "Employees Turn to the Informal Organization." *Strategic Finance* (September 2007): 17.

14. Neil Farmer, *The Invisible Organization: How Informal Networks Can Lead Organizational Change* (Surrey, United Kingdom: Gower Publishing, 2008).

15. Neil Farmer, *The Invisible Organization.*

Chapter 3

1. Rodney Dangerfield, *Back to School,* movie, directed by Alan Metter (Los Angeles: Orion, 1986).

2. Michael Ba Banutu-Gomez, "Great Leaders Teach Exemplary Followership and Serve as Servant Leaders," *The Journal of American Academy of Business, Cambridge* (March 2004): 143–151; Patsy B. Blackshear, "The Followership Continuum: A Model for Fine Tuning the Workforce," *Public Manager* 32, no. 2 (2003): 25–29; Larry Bossidy, "What Your Leader Expects of You," *Harvard Business Review* 85, no. 4 (2007): 58–65; David P. Cavell, "Leadership or Followership: One or Both?" *Healthcare Financial Management,* (November 2007): 142–144; William J. Crockett, "Dynamic Subordinancy," *Training and Development Journal* (May 1981): 155–164; Miguel Pina Cunha et al., "The Case for Transcendent Followership," *Leadership* 9, no. 1 (1981): 87–106; Olga Epitropaki et al., "Implicit Leadership and Followership Theories 'in the Wild': Taking Stock of Information-Processing Approaches to Leadership and Followership in Organizational Settings," *The Leadership Quarterly* 24 (2013): 858–881; Mary K. Guidera and Christine Gilmore, "Working with People: In Defense of Followership," *The American Journal of Nursing* 88, no. 7 (1988): 1017; Marc Hurwitz and Samantha Hurwitz, "The Romance of the Follower: Part 2," *Industrial and Commercial Training* 41, no. 4 (2009): 199–206; Barbara Kellerman, *Followership: How Followers Are Creating Change and Changing Leaders* (Boston: Harvard Business Press, 2009); Robert E. Kelley, "In Praise of Followers," *Harvard Business Review* (November 1988): 142–148; Robert E. Kelley, *The Power of Followership* (New York: Doubleday, 1992); Sharon M. Latour

and Vicki J. Rast, "Dynamic Followership: The Prerequisite for Effective Leadership," *Air & Space Power Journal* (Winter 2004): 102–110; Ronald Lippitt, "The Changing Leader-Follower Relationships of the 1980s," *The Journal of Applied Behavioral Science* 18, no. 3 (1982): 395–403; Stephen C. Lundin and Lynne C. Lancaster, "The Importance of Followership," *The Futurist* (May 1990): 18–22; Kurt Madden, *The Synergetic Follower: Changing Our World without Becoming the Leader*, (United States: Kurt Madden, 2011); Bruno Neal, "Heroes and Sidekicks: Ensuring Proper Followership," *T+D* (September 2010): 76–77; James S. Nolan and Henry F. Harty, "Followership ≥ Leadership," *Education* 104, no. 3 (2001): 311–312; Burak Oc and Michael R. Bashshur, "Followership, Leadership and Social Influence," *The Leadership Quarterly* 24 (2013): 919–934; William E. Rosenbach, Thane S. Pittman, and Earl H. Potter III, "What Makes a Follower?" *Contemporary Issues in Leadership* (2012): 77–87; Alden Solovy, "Followership," *Hospitals and Health Networks* 79, no. 5 (2005): 32; Angela Thody, "Followership in Educational Organizations: A Pilot Mapping of the Territory," *Leadership and Policy in Schools* 2, no. 2 (2003): 141–156; Alan Wilson, *Attaining Peak Performance* (Cardiff, Wales: 1000 Lives Plus, 2012).

3. Paul Berg, "The Importance of Teaching Followership in Professional Military Education," *Military Review* 94, no. 5 (2014): 65–71; Kent Bjugstad et al., "A Fresh Look at Followership: A Model for Matching Followership and Leadership Styles," *Journal of Behavioral and Applied Management* 7.3 (2006): 304–319; Abdullah Can and Mert Aktaş, "Cultural Values and Followership Style Preferences," *Procedia-Social and Behavioral Sciences* 41 (2012): 84–91; Ira Chaleff, *The Courageous Follower: Standing Up To & For Our Leaders* (San Francisco: Berrett-Koehler, 2009); Oc and Bashshur, "Followership, Leadership"; Thody, "Followership in Educational Organizations."

4. A study-by-study presentation of the qualities of the ideal follower reported in the descriptive literature can be found at http://nbaldwin .people.ua.edu/uploads/9/6/0/3/96039570/follower_ideal_qualities_by _study.pdf.

5. A study-by-study presentation of the findings from the empirical research on the qualities of the ideal follower can be found at http:// nbaldwin.people.ua.edu/uploads/9/6/0/3/96039570/follower_ideal _qualities_research_based.pdf.

6. Augustine O. Agho, "Perspectives of Senior-Level Executives on Effective Followership," *Journal of Leadership & Organizational Studies* 16, no. 2 (2009): 159–166; David S. Alcorn, "Dynamic Followership: Empowerment at Work," *Management Quarterly* 33, no. 1

(1992): 9–13; Melissa K. Carsten et al., "Exploring Social Construc-
tions of Followership: A Qualitative Study," *The Leadership Quarterly*
21 (2010): 543–562; Frederic Damen, Barbara van Knippenberg, and
Daan van Knippenberg, "Affective Match in Leadership: Leader Emo-
tional Displays, Follower Positive Affect, and Follower Performance,"
Journal of Applied Social Psychology 38, no. 4 (2008): 868–902; Ronald
G. Gilbert and Albert C. Hyde, "Followership and the Federal Worker,"
Public Administration Review, November (1988a): 962–968; Ronald G.
Gilbert and Carl W. Whiteside, "Performance Appraisal and Follower-
ship: An Analysis of the Officer on the Boss/Subordinate Team," *Journal
of Police Science and Administration* 16, no. 1 (1988): 39–43; Susan E.
Murphy and Ellen A. Ensher, "The Effects of Leader and Subordinate
Characteristics in the Development of Leader-Member Exchange Qual-
ity," *Journal of Applied Social Psychology* 29, no. 7 (1999): 1371–1394;
Thomas Sy, "What Do You Think of Followers: Examining the Content,
Structure, and Consequences of Implicit Followership Theories," *Organ-
izational Behavior and Human Decision Processes* 113 (2010): 73–84;
Gerben A. van Kleef et al., "Searing Sentiment or Cold Calculation: The
Effects of Leader Emotional Displays on Team Performance Depend on
Follower Epistemic Motivation," *Academy of Management Journal* 52,
no. 3 (2009): 562–580; Gerben A. van Kleef et al., "On Angry Lead-
ers and Agreeable Followers: How Leaders' Emotions and Followers'
Personalities Shape Motivation and Team Performance," *Psychological
Science* 21, no. 12 (2010): 1827–1834; Paul Whiteley, Thomas Sy, and
Stefanie K. Johnson, "Leaders' Conceptions of Followers: Implications
for Naturally Occurring Pygmalion Effects," *The Leadership Quarterly*
23 (2012): 822–834.

 7. Susan D. Baker, Christopher J. Mathis, and Susan Stites-Doe, "An
Exploratory Study Investigating Leader and Follower Characteristics
at U.S. Healthcare Organizations," *Journal of Managerial Issues* XXIII,
no. 3 (2011): 341–363; Jennie Billot et al., "Followership in Higher
Education: Academic Teachers and Their Formal Leaders," *Teaching
and Learning Inquiry* 1, no. 2 (2013): 91–103; Anita L. Blanchard et al.,
"Followership Styles and Employee Attachment to the Organization,"
The Psychologist-Manager Journal 12 (2009): 111–131; Melissa K.
Carsten and Mary Uhl-Bien, "Follower Beliefs in the Co-production of
Leadership," *Zeitschrift für Psychologie* 220, no. 4 (2012): 210–220;
Melissa K. Carsten and Mary Uhl-Bien, "Ethical Followership: An
Examination of Followership Beliefs and Crimes of Obedience," *Jour-
nal of Leadership & Organizational Studies* 20, no. 1 (2013): 49–61;
Nai-Wen Chi and Ta-Rui Ho, "Understanding When Leader Negative

Emotional Expression Enhances Follower Performance: The Moderating Roles of Follower Personality Traits and Perceived Leader Power," *Human Relations* 67, no. 9 (2014): 1051–1072; Robert L. Heneman and Debra J. Cohen, "Supervisory and Employee Characteristics as Correlates of Employee Salary Increases," *Personnel Psychology* 41, no. 2 (1988): 345–360; Elizabeth W. Morrison and Corey C. Phelps, "Taking Charge at Work: Extrarole Efforts to Initiate Workplace Change," *Academy of Management Journal* 42, no. 4 (1999): 403–419; Antoinette S. Phillips and Arthur G. Bedeian, "Leader-Follower Exchange Quality: The Role of Personal and Interpersonal Attributes," *Academy of Management Journal* 37, no. 4 (1994): 990–1001; Benson Rosen and Thomas H. Jerdee, "Influence of Subordinate Characteristics on Trust and Use of Participative Decision Strategies in a Management Simulation," *Journal of Applied Psychology* 62, no. 5 (1977): 628–631; Birgit Schyns and Jörg Felfe, "The Personality of Followers and Its Effect on the Perception of Leadership," *Small Group Research* 37, no. 5 (2006): 522–539; Victoria Visser et al., "How Leader Displays of Happiness and Sadness Influence Follower Performance: Emotional Contagion and Creative Versus Analytical Performance," *The Leadership Quarterly* 24 (2013): 172–188; Barbara Wisse and Eric Rietzschel, "Humor in Leader-Follower Relationships: Humor Styles, Similarity, and Relationship Quality," *Humor* 27, no. 2 (2014): 249–269; Seokhwa Yun, Jonathan Cox, and Henry P. Sims Jr, "The Forgotten Follower: A Contingency Model of Leadership and Follower Self-Leadership," *Journal of Managerial Psychology* 21, no. 4 (2006): 374–388; Weichun Zhu, Bruce J. Avolio, and Fred O. Walumbwa, "Moderating Role of Follower Characteristics with Transformational Leadership and Follower Work Engagement," *Group & Organization Management* 34, no. 5 (2009): 590–619.

8. The synonyms for agreeable are the easiest to debate. One might argue that followers can be cooperative, obedient, and non-questioning, even though they may not agree with management.

9. One might also argue that competency does not drop out as a leading quality of ideal followers because being an effective communicator and interpersonally skillful are subcategories of competency.

10. Agho, "Perspectives of Senior-Level Executives"; Alcorn, "Dynamic Followership"; Gilbert and Hyde, "Followership and the Federal Worker"; Gilbert and Whiteside, "Performance Appraisal"; Sy, "What Do You Think"; Whitely et al., "Leaders' Conceptions."

11. Because they appear once or twice as ideal follower qualities in the most rigorous quantitative studies, I believe the following should be

given special attention in future followership research: enthusiasm, good citizenship, loyalty, problem-solver, proper comportment, and sense of humor. Cooperation could be added to this list unless one believes it should be grouped with the synonyms associated with being agreeable or a team player.

Chapter 4

1. Chris Jernigan, in discussion with the author, August 30, 2016.

2. The old Chris would offer you, the reader, the opportunity to meet him in some bar or club where he could take center stage and capture your attention, laughs, and adoration for the sole purpose of satisfying his ego. The new Chris has literally asked me to tell you that if you ever need help, support, comfort, or advice, he would like to be there for you.

3. Ryan Cooper, *Habit Change Now: The Ultimate Guide to Changing Any Habit Fast* (2014a), Kindle, https://www.amazon.com/gp/product /B00KSP4CBK/ref=kinw_myk_ro_title; Robin Madison, *How to Change Your Life: Making a Personal Transformation* (2014), Kindle, https:// www.amazon.com/gp/product/B00G13BHHU/ref=kinw_myk_ro_title.

4. Justin Albert, *A Practical Guide to Unleash Your True Potential* (2013), Kindle, https://www.amazon.com/gp/product/B00JBNXQ2G/ref= kinw_myk_ro_title; Seth Cohen, *Willpower Workout: How to Successfully Strengthen Your Self Discipline & Boost Self Control* (2014), Kindle, https://kindle.amazon.com/work/willpower-workout--strengthen -discipline-ebook/B00IRHOOI2/B00IMW0Q2U; Ryan Cooper, *Self Discipline: The Ultimate Guide to Self-Discipline,* (2014b), Kindle, https://www.amazon.com/gp/product/B00KNEU7O2/ref=kinw_myk _ro_title; Charles Duhigg, *The Power of Habit: A Full Summary* (2015), Kindle, https://www.amazon.com/Power-Habit-Charles-Business-Audio book-ebook/dp/B018F1SB5Q/ref=sr_1_2?ie=UTF8&qid=1466874948 &sr=8-2&keywords=duhigg+power+habit; Jeffrey A. Kottler, *Change: What Really Leads to Personal Transformation* (New York, NY: Oxford University Press, 2014); Robin Madison, *How to Change Your Life*; Patterson et al., *Change Anything: A New Science of Personal Success* (New York, NY: Business Plus, 2011); Matt Price, *Personal Transformation Map. The Ultimate and Easy Way to Move from Where You Are to Where You Want to Be* (2014), Kindle, https://www.amazon.com/gp /product/B00F94TLS4/ref=kinw_myk_ro_title; Daniel J. Siegel, *Mindsight: The New Science of Personal Transformation* (New York: Bantam Books, 2011).

5. Steven Covey, *The 7 Habits of Highly Effective People* (New York: Fireside Books, 1989).

6. Price, *Personal Transformation Map*.

7. David C. McClelland, *Human Motivation* (New York, NY: Cambridge University Press, 1989).

8. Patterson et al., *Change Anything*.

9. Change Anything Lab, *Friends and Accomplices* (Provo, UT: Change Anything Lab, 2009).

10. Paul F. Wernimont and John P. Campbell, "Signs, Samples, and Criteria," *Journal of Applied Psychology* 52 (1968): 372–376.

11. Vince Lombardi, BrainyQuote.com, http://www.brainyquote.com/quotes/quotes/v/vincelomba138158.html.

12. Kottler, *Change, What Really Happens*, 202.

13. Siegel, *Mindsight*, 34, 97.

14. Cooper, *Habit Change Now*; Cohen, *Willpower Workout*; Duhigg, *The Power of Habit*; Kottler, *Change, What Really Happens*.

15. Patterson et al., *Change Anything*, 32.

16. Patterson et al., *Change Anything*, IX, Part 2.

17. Patterson et al., *Change Anything*, 106.

18. Don Novello, *Father Guido Sarducci's Five Minute University*, YouTube Video File, posted by messi19azzurtina Jan 23, 2007, https://www.youtube.com/watch?v=kO8x8eoU3L4.

19. National Center for Education Statistics, "Characteristics of Degree-Granting Postsecondary Institutions," http://nces.ed.gov/programs/coe/indicator_csa.asp.

20. U.S. Bureau of Census, "How Many People Reside in Urban and Rural Areas for the 2010 Census? What Percentage of the Population Is Urban or Rural?" accessed June 21, 2015, https://ask.census.gov/faq.php?id=5000&fa.

21. Online Course Report, "State of the MOOC 2016: A Year of Massive Landscape Change for the Massive Open Online Courses," accessed June 22, 2016, www.ursereport.com/state-of-the-016-a-year-of-massive-landscape-change-for-massive-open-online-courses/onlinecomooc-2.

22. Coursera, "Courses and Specializations: Communication Skills," accessed August 23, 2016, https://www.coursera.org/courses?languages=en&query=communications+skills; Coursera, "Courses and Specializations: Interpersonal Skills," accessed August 23, 2016, https://www.coursera.org/courses?languages=en&query=interpersonal+skills; edX, "Courses Communications Skills," accessed August 23, 2016, https://www.edx.org/course?search_query=communication+skills; edX, "Courses Interpersonal Skills," accessed August 23, 2016, https://www.edx.org/course?search_query=Interpersonal+skills.

23. MOOC List, "MOOC List: Communications Skills," accessed August 23, 2016, https://cse.google.com/cse?cx=partner-pub-61297257

06670587:7768334159&ie=UTF-8&q=communication+skills&sa
=Search&ref=www.google.com/#gsc.tab=0&gsc.q=communication
%20skills&gsc.page=1; Mooc List, "Mooc List: Interpersonal Skills,"
accessed August 23, 2016, https://cse.google.com/cse?cx=partner-pub
-6129725706670587:7768334159&ie=UTF-8&q=interpersonal+skills
&sa=Search&ref=www.google.com/#gsc.tab=0&gsc.q=interpersonal
%20skills&gsc.page=1.

Chapter 5

1. Patsy B. Blackshear, "The Followership Continuum: A Model for
Increasing Organization Productivity," *The Public Sector Innovation
Journal 9*, no. 1 (2004): 2–16; James M. Burns, *Leadership*, (New York:
Harper & Row, 1978); Melissa K. Carsten, "Exploring Social Construc-
tions of Followership: A Qualitative Study," *The Leadership Quarterly*
21 (2010): 543–562; Ira Chaleff, *The Courageous Follower: Standing
Up To and For Our Leaders* (San Francisco: Berrett-Koehler, 2009);
David Collinson, "Rethinking Followership: A Post-Structuralist Analy-
sis of Follower Identities," *The Leadership Quarterly* 17 (2006): 179–
189; David Collinson, "Conformist, Resistant, and Disguised Selves: A
Post-Structuralist Approach to Identity and Workplace Followership,"
in the *Art of Followership*, ed. Ronald E. Riggio, Ira Chaleff, and Jean
Lipman-Blumen (San Francisco: Jossey-Bass, 2008); Epitropaki et al.,
"Implicit Leadership and Followership Theories 'in the Wild': Taking
Stock of Information-Processing Approaches to Leadership and Followership in Organizational Settings," *The Leadership Quarterly* 24 (2013):
858–881; John P. Howell and Maria Mendez, "Three Perspectives on
Followership," in *The Art of Followership*, ed. Riggio et al. (San Francisco: Jossey-Bass, 2008); Kimberly S. Jaussi, Andy Stefanovich, and
Patricia G. Devlin, "Effective Followership for Creativity and Innova-
tion: A Range of Colors and Dimensions," in *The Art of Followership*,
ed. Riggio et al. (San Francisco: Jossey-Bass, 2008); Barbara Kellerman,
Followership (Review Press, 2008); Robert E. Kelley, *The Power of Fol-
lowership* (New York: Doubleday Currency, 1992); Robert E. Kelley,
"Rethinking Followership," in *The Art of Followership*, ed. Riggio et al.
(San Francisco: Jossey-Bass, 2008); Sharon M. Latour and Vicki J. Rast,
"Dynamic Followership: The Prerequisite for Effective Leadership," *Air
and Space Journal* (Winter 2004): 102–110; Jean Lipman-Blumen, *The
Allure of Toxic Leaders* (New York: Oxford University Press, 2005);
Kurt Madden, *The Synergetic Follower: Changing the World without
Being the Leader* (North Charleston SC: Createspace, 2011); William E.

Rosenbach, Thane S. Pittman, and Earl H. Potter, "What Makes a Follower?" in *Contemporary Issues in Leadership*, 7th ed., ed. William E. Rosenbach, Robert L. Taylor, and Mark A. Youndt (Boulder, CO: Westview, 2012); Boas Shamir, "Followers, Motivation Of," in *Encyclopedia of Leadership*, ed. George R. Goethals, Georgia J. Sorensen, and James M. Burns (Thousand Oaks, CA: Sage, 2004); Boas Shamir, "From Passive Recipient to Active Co-Producer," in *Follower Centered Perspective on Leadership: A Tribute to the Memory of James R. Meindl*, ed. Boas Shamir et al. (Greenwich CT: Information Age Publishing, 2007); Joseph A. Steger, George E. Manners Jr., and Thomas Zimmerer, "Following the Leader: How to Link Management Style to Subordinate Personalities," *Management Review* 17, no. 10 (1982): 22–31; Thomas Sy, "What Do You Think of Followers? Examining the Content, Structure, and Consequences of Implicit Followership Theories," *Organizational Behavior and Human Decision Processes* 113 (2010): 73–84; Abraham Zaleznik, "The Dynamics of Subordinacy," *Harvard Business Review* 43, no. 3 (1965): 119–131.

2. Ideally, a parsimonious set of followership styles would be developed through surveying several thousand random followers and factor analyzing answers to operationalizations of the 90 followership types.

Chapter 6

1. Kim S. Cameron and Robert E. Quinn, *Diagnosing and Changing Organizational Culture Based on the Competing Values Framework*, 3rd ed. (San Francisco: Jossey-Bass, 2011); Sai O. Cheung, Peter S. P. Wong, and Tak W. Yiu, "Exploring Organisational Culture-Performance Relationship in Construction," in *The Soft Power of Construction Contracting Organisation*, ed. Sao O. Cheung, Peter S. P. Wong, Tak W. Yiu, and K. Y. Lamb (New York: Routledge, 2015), 19–37; James R. Detert, Roger G. Schroeder, and John J. Mauriel, "A Framework for Linking Culture and Improvement Initiatives in Organizations," *Academy of Management Review* 25, no. 4 (2000): 850–863; H. Kirk Downey, Don Hellriegel, and John W. Slocum Jr., "Congruence between Individual Needs, Organizational Climate, Job Satisfaction and Performance," *Academy of Management Journal* 18, no. 1 (1974): 149–155; Richard E. Kopelman, Arthur P. Brief, and Richard A. Guzzo, "The Role of Climate and Culture in Productivity," in *Organization Climate and Culture*, ed. Benjamin S. Schneider (San Francisco: Jossey-Bass, 1999), 282–318; George H. Litwin and Robert Stringer, *Motivation and Organization Climate* (Cambridge, MA: Harvard University Press, 1968); Charles

A. O'Reilly III, Jennifer Chatman, and David F. Caldwell, "People and Organizational Culture: A Profile Comparison Approach to Assessing Person-Organization Fit," *Academy of Management Journal* 34 (1991): 487–516; Udai Pareek, *Training Instrument in HRD and OD*, 2nd ed. (New Delhi: Tata McGraw-Hill Publishing, 2002); Robert E. Quinn and John Rohrbaugh, "Spatial Model of Effectiveness Criteria: Towards a Competing Values Approach to Organizational Analysis," *Management Science* 29 (1983): 363–377; James C. Taylor and David G. Bowers, *Survey of Organizations: A Machine-Scored Standardized Questionnaire Instrument* (Ann Arbor, MI: Center for Research on Utilization of Scientific Knowledge, the University of Michigan, 1972).

2. Daniel R. Denison, "What Is the Difference between Organizational Culture and Organizational Climate? A Native's Point of View on a Decade of Paradigm Wars," *Academy of Management Review* 21, no. 3 (1996): 619–654; Joan R. Rentsch, "Climate and Culture: Interaction and Qualitative Differences in Organizational Meanings," *Journal of Applied Psychology* 75, no. 6 (1990): 668–681; Benjamin Schneider, Mark G. Ehrhart, and William H. Macey, "Organization Culture and Climate," *Annual Review of Psychology* 64 (2013): 361–388; Willem Verbeke, Marco Volgering, and Marco Hessels, "Exploring the Conceptual Expansion within the Field of Organizational Behavior: Organizational Climate and Organizational Culture," *Journal of Management Studies* 35, no. 3 (2014): 303–329.

3. David Needle, *Business in Context: An Introduction to Business and Its Environment* (London: Thomson, 2004); David Ravasi and Majken Schultz, "Responding to Organizational Identity Threats: Exploring the Role of Organizational Culture," *Academy of Management Journal* 49, no. 3 (2006): 433–458; Denise M. Rousseau, "Assessing Organizational Culture: The Case for Multiple Methods," in *Organizational Climate and Culture*, ed. Benjamin Schneider (San Francisco: Jossey-Bass, 1990), 153–192; Schneider et al., "Organization Culture."

4. Denison, "What Is the Difference"; William F. Joyce and John W. Slocum, "Correlations of Climate Discrepancies," *Human Relations* 35 (1982): 951–972; William F. Joyce and John W. Slocum, "Collective Climate: Agreement as Basis for Defining Aggregate Climates in Organizations," *Academy of Management Journal* 27, no. 4 (1984): 721; Karen Meudell and Karen Gadd, "Culture and Climate in Short Life Organizations: Sunny Spells or Thunderstorms? *International Journal of Contemporary Hospitality Management* 6, no. 5 (1994): 28; Schneider

et al., "Organization Culture"; Benjamin Schneider and Arnon E. Reichers, "On the Etiology of Climates," *Personnel Psychology* 36 (1983): 19–39.

5. Mian M. Ajmal and Kay U. Koskinen, "Knowledge Transfer in Project-Based Organizations: An Organizational Culture Perspective," *Project Management Journal* 39, no. 1 (2008): 7–15.

6. Frederick Mosher, *Democracy and the Public Service* (London: Oxford Press, 1982).

Chapter 7

1. Chris Argyris, *Integrating the Individual and the Organization* (New York: Wiley, 1964); Frederick Herzberg, "One More Time: How Do You Motivate Employees?" *Harvard Business Review* 65, no. 5 (1987): 109–120; Abraham Maslow, "A Theory of Human Motivation." *Psychological Review* 50 (1943): 370–396; Douglas McGregor, *The Human Side of Enterprise* (New York, McGraw-Hill, 1987).

2. Nicole M. Kierein and Michael A. Gold, "Pygmalion in Work Organizations: A Meta-analysis." *Journal of Organizational Behaviour* 21 (2000): 913–928; Brian McNatt, "Ancient Pygmalion Joins Contemporary Management: A Meta-Analysis of the Result," *Journal of Applied Psychology* 85, no. 2 (2000): 314–322.

3. Joseph Sarros et al. "Work Alienation and Organizational Leadership," *British Journal of Management* 13 (2002): 285–304.

4. Benjamin M. Bloom et al., *Taxonomy of Educational Objectives: The Classification of Educational Goals, Handbook I. Cognitive Domain* (New York: Longmans, Green, 1957).

5. Toyohiko Kagawa, *Living Out Christ's Love: Selected Writings of Toyokiko Kagawa,* ed. Keith Beasley-Topliffe (Nashville: Upper Room Books, 1998).

6. Robert K. Merton, *Social Theory and Social Structure* (Glencoe, IL: Free Press, 1957); Victor A. Thompson, *Without Sympathy or Enthusiasm: A Problem of Administrative Compassion* (Tuscaloosa, AL: University of Alabama Press, 1975).

7. M. Scott Peck, *The Road Less Travelled* (New York: Touchstone Books, 1978).

8. Lydia Saad, *The "40-Hour" Workweek Is Actually Longer—By Seven Hours*, accessed January 19, 2015, http://www.gallup.com/poll/175286/hour-workweek-actually-longer-seven-hours.aspx.

Chapter 8

1. A study-by-study presentation of the findings from the 19 meta-analyses predicting job satisfaction in a cross section of organizations can be found at http://nbaldwin.people.ua.edu/uploads/9/6/0/3/96039570/follower_appendix_8.1_web.pdf. The references for these studies are as follows: David J. Abrams, "Work Role Ambiguity, Job Satisfaction, and Job Performance: Meta-Analyses and Review," *Psychological Reports* 75 (1994): 1411–1433; Bal et al., "Psychological Contract Breach and Job Attitudes: A Meta-Analysis of Age as a Moderator," *Journal of Vocational Behavior* 72 (2008): 143–158; Gabriela T. Cantisano, Morales Dominguez, and Marco Depolo, "Psychological Contract Breach and Outcomes: Combining Meta-Analysis and Structural Equation Models," *Psicothema* 20, no. 3 (2008): 487–497; Yochi Cohen-Charash and Paul E. Spector, "The Role of Justice in Organizations: A Meta-Analysis. Organizational Behavior and Human Decision Processes," *Organizational Behavior and Human Decision Processes* 86, no. 2 (2001): 278–321; Anne L. Davis and Hannah R. Rothstein, "The Effects of the Perceived Behavioral Integrity of Managers on Employee Attitudes: A Meta-Analysis," *Journal of Business Ethics* 67 (2006): 407–419; Yitzhak Fried et al., "The Mediating Effects of Job Satisfaction and Propensity to Leave on Role Stress-Job Performance Relationships: Combing Meta-Analysis and Structural Equation Modeling," *International Journal of Stress Management* 15, no. 4 (2008): 305–328; Rajash Ghosh and Thomas G. Reio Jr., "Career Benefits Associated with Mentoring for Mentors: A Meta-Analysis," *Journal of Vocational Behavior* 83, no. 1 (2013): 106–116; Timothy A. Judge et al., "The Relationship between Pay and Job Satisfaction: A Meta-Analysis," *Journal of Vocational Behavior* 77 (2010): 157–167; Dorien T. A. M. Kooij et al., "The Influence of Age on the Associations between HR Practices and Both Affective Commitment and Job Satisfaction: A Meta-Analysis," *Journal of Organizational Behavior* 31 (2010): 1111–1136; Ellen E. Kossek and Cynthia Ozeki, "Work-Family Conflict, Policies, and the Job-Life Satisfaction Relationship: A Review and Directions for Organizational Behavior-Human Resources Research," *Journal of Applied Psychology* 83, no. 2 (1998): 139–149; Jaana Kuoppala et al., "Leadership, Job Well-being, and Health Effects—A Systematic Review and Meta-Analysis," *Journal of Occupational and Environmental Management* 50, no. 8 (2008): 904–913; Laurent M. Lapierre, Paul Spector, and Joanne D. Leck; "Sexual Versus Nonsexual Workplace Aggression and Victims Overall Job Satisfaction: A Meta-Analysis," *Journal of Occupational Health Psychology* 10, no. 3 (2005): 155–169; Brian T. Loher

and Raymond A. Noe, "A Meta-Analysis of the Relation of Job Characteristics to Job Satisfaction," *Journal of Applied Psychology* 70, no. 1 (1985): 280–289; Brian K. Miller, Matthew A. Rutherford, and Robert W. Kolodinsky, "Perceptions of Organizational Politics: A Meta-Analysis of Outcome," *Journal of Business Psychology* 22 (2008): 209–222; Robert J. Riggle, Diane R. Edmondson, and John D. Hansen, "A Meta-Analysis of the Relationship between Perceived Organizational Support and Job Outcomes: 20 Years of Research," *Journal of Business Research* 62 (2009): 1027–1030; Chet Robie et al., "The Relation Between Job Level and Job Satisfaction," *Group and Organization Management* 23, no. 4 (1998): 470–495; Paul E. Spector, "Higher-Order Need Strength as a Moderator of the Job Scope-Employee Outcome Relationship: A Meta-Analysis," *Journal of Occupational Psychology* 58 (1985): 119–127; Michelle L. Verquer, Terry A. Beehr, and Stephen H. Wagner, "A Meta-Analysis of Relations between Person-Organization Fit and Work Attitudes," *Journal of Vocational Behavior* 63 (2003): 473–489; Christa L. Wilkin, "I Can't Get No Job Satisfaction: Meta-Analysis Comparing Permanent and Contingent Worker." *Journal of Organizational Behavior* 34 (2013): 47–64; Alan L. Witt and Lendell G. Nye, "Gender and the Relationship between Perceived Fairness of Pay or Promotion and Job Satisfaction," *Journal of Applied Psychology* 77, no. 6 (1992): 910–917.

2. A study-by-study presentation of the findings from the 11 meta-analyses predicting job satisfaction in specific occupations can be found at http://nbaldwin.people.ua.edu/uploads/9/6/0/3/96039570 /follower_appendix_8.2_web.pdf. The references for these studies are as follows: Ayhan Aydin, Yilmaz Sarier, and Sengul Uysal, "The Effect of Gender on Job Satisfaction of Teachers: A Meta-Analysis Study," *Procedia–Social and Behavioral Sciences* 46 (2012): 356–362; Ayhan Aydin, Yilmaz Sarier, and Sengul Uysal, "The Effect of School Principals' Leadership Styles on Teachers' Organizational Commitment and Job Satisfaction," *Educational Sciences: Theory & Practice* 13, no. 2 (2013): 806–811; John A. Brierley, "Accountants' Job Satisfaction: A Meta-Analysis," *British Accounting Review* 31 (1999): 63–84; Steven P. Brown and Robert A. Peterson, "Antecedents and Consequences of Salesperson Job Satisfaction: Metal-Analysis and Assessment of Causal Effects," *Journal of Marketing Research* 30, no. 1 (1993): 63–77; George R. Franke and Jeong-Eun Park, "Salesperson Adaptive Selling Behavior and Customer Orientation: A Meta-Analysis," *Journal of Marketing Research* 43 (November 2006): 693–702; Denise K. Gromley, "Factors Affecting Job Satisfaction in Nurse Faculty: A Meta-Analysis,"

Journal of Nursing Education 42, no. 4 (2003): 174–178; Deborah Saber, "Frontline Registered Nurse Job Satisfaction and Predictors over Three Decades: A Meta-Analysis from 1980 to 2009," *Nursing Outlook* 62 (2014): 402–414; Yide Shen, "A Meta-Analysis of Role Ambiguity and Role Conflict on IS Professional Job Satisfaction," in *Proceeding of the 38th Hawaii International Conference on Systems Sciences*, Manoa, Hawaii, January 3–6 (Washington, DC: IEEE Computer Society, 2005), 1–11; Shir G. Toh, Emily Ang, and M. Kamala Devi, "Systematic Review on the Relationship between the Nursing Shortage and Job Satisfaction, Stress, and Burnout Levels among Nurses in Oncology/Haematology Settings," *International Journal of Evidence-Based Healthcare* 10 (2012): 126–141; David P. Thompson, James F. McNamara, and John R. Hoyle, "Job Satisfaction in Educational Organizations: A Synthesis of Research Findings," *Educational Administrative Quarterly* 33, no. 1 (1977): 7–37; Richard W. Vanvoorhis and Edward M. Levinson, "Job Satisfaction among School Psychologists: A Meta-Analysis," *School Psychology Quarterly* 21, no. 1 (2006): 77–90; George A. Zangaro and Karen L. Soeken, "A Meta-Analysis of Studies of Nurses' Job Satisfaction," *Research in Nursing and Health* 30 (2007): 445–458.

3. A study-by-study presentation of the findings from the 15 meta-analyses predicting job satisfaction based on the nature and values of employees can be found at http://nbaldwin.people.ua.edu /uploads/9/6/0/3/96039570/follower_appendix_8.3_web.pdf. The references for these studies are as follows: Brierley, "Accountants' Job Satisfaction"; Nathan A. Bowling et al., "A Meta-Analysis of the Predictors and Consequences of Organization-Based Self-Esteem," *Journal of Occupational and Organizational Psychology* 83 (2010): 601–626; Valentina Bruk-Lee et al., "Replicating and Extending Post Personality/Job Satisfaction Meta-Analyses," *Human Performance* 22 (2009): 156–189; Donald Brush, Michael K. Moch, and Abdullah Pooyan, "Individual Demographic Differences and Job Satisfaction," *Journal of Occupational Behavior (1986–1998)* 8, no. 2 (1987): 139–155; James J. Connolly and Chockalingam Visweswaran, "The Role of Affectivity in Job Satisfaction: A Meta-Analysis," *Personality and Individual Differences* 29 (2000): 265–281; David P. Constanza et al., "Generational Differences in Work-related Attitudes: A Meta-Analysis," *Journal of Business Psychology* 27 (2012): 375–394; Carol Dole and Richard G. Schroeder, "The Impact of Various Factors on the Personality, Job Satisfaction, and Turnover Intentions of Professional Accountants," *Managerial Auditing Journal* 14, no. 4 (2001): 234–245; Timothy Judge and Joyce E. Bono, "Relationship

of Core Self-Evaluations Traits—Self-Esteem, Generalized Self-Efficacy, Locus of Control, and Emotional Stability—With Job Satisfaction and Job Performance: A Meta-Analysis," *Journal of Applied Psychology* 86, no. 1 (2001): 80–92; Timothy A. Judge, Daniel Heller, and Michael K. Mount, "Five-factor Model of Personality and Job Satisfaction: A Meta-Analysis," *Journal of Applied Psychology* 87, no. 3 (2002): 530–341; Seth A. Kaplan, Christopher R. Warren, Adam P. Barsky, and Carl J. Thoresen, "A Note on the Relationship between Affect(ivity) and Differing Conceptualizations of Job Satisfaction: Some Unexpected Findings," *European Journal of Work and Organizational Psychology* 18, no. 1 (2009): 29–54; Chloe J. Lemelle and Shannon A. Scielzo, "How You Feel about Yourself Can Affect How You Feel about Your Job: A Meta-Analysis Examining the Relationship of Core Self-evaluations and Job Satisfaction," *Journal of Business Diversity* 12, no. 3 (2012): 116–133; Deo J. W. Strumpfer, "Antonovsky's Sense of Coherence and Job Satisfaction: Meta-Analyses of South African Data," *SA Journal of Industrial Psychology* 35, no. 1 (2009): 172–174; Marianne Tait, Margaret Y. Padgett, and Timothy T. Baldwin, "Job and Life Satisfaction: A reevaluation of the Strength of the Relationship and Gender Effects as a Function of the Date of the Study," *Journal of Applied Psychology* 74, no. 3 (1989): 502–507; Jeffrey P. Thomas, Daniel S. Whitman, and Chockalingam Viswesvaran, "Employee Proactivity in Organizations: A Comparative Meta-Analysis of Emergent Proactive Constructs," *Journal of Occupational and Organizational Psychology* 83 (2010): 275–300; L. Alan Witt and Lendell G. Nye, "Gender and the Relationship between Perceived Fairness of Pay or Promotion and Job Satisfaction," *Journal of Applied Psychology* 77, no. 6 (1992): 910–917.

4. Cohen-Charash and Paul E. Spector, "The Role of Justice," 280.

5. Cohen-Charash and Paul E. Spector, "The Role of Justice," 280–281.

6. Davis et al., "The Effects of the Perceived Behavioral Integrity."

7. Riggle et al., "A Meta-Analysis of the Relationship," 1027.

8. Amy L. Kristof, "Person–Organization Fit: An Integrative Review of Its Conceptualizations, Measurement, and Implications," *Personnel Psychology* 49, no. 1 (1996): 4–5.

9. Organizational politics has an especially negative effect on the job satisfaction of ethnic and international employees.

10. In particular, women experience a diminution of job satisfaction when they experience non-sexual aggression.

11. Miller et al., "Perceptions of Organizational Politics," 209.

12. Miller et al., "Perceptions of Organizational Politics."

13. Susan E. Jackson and Randal S. Schuler, "A Meta-Analysis and Conceptual Critique of Research on Role Ambiguity and Role Conflict in Work Settings," *Organizational Behavior and Human Decision Processes* 36, no. 1 (1985): 16–78.

14. Bal et al., "Psychological Contract Breach."

15. Lapierre et al., "Sexual Versus Nonsexual Workplace."

16. J. Richard Hackman et al., "A New Strategy for Job Enrichment," *California Management Review* 17, no. 4 (1975): 57–71.

17. Joanne Terrell, in discussion with the author, August 29, 2016.

18. Christian Dormann and Dieter Zapf, "Job Satisfaction: A Meta-Analysis of Stabilities," *Journal of Organizational Behavior* 22 (2001): 483–504.

19. Bruk-Lee et al., "Replicating and Extending Post Personality/Job Satisfaction."

20. Kaplan et al., "A Note on the Relationship," 33; David Watson and Lee A. Clark, "Negative Affectivity: The Disposition to Experience Aversive Emotional States," *Psychological Bulletin* 96, no. 3 (1984): 465–490.

21. Felix Cheung and Richard E. Lucas, "When Does Money Matter Most? Examining the Association between Income and Life Satisfaction over the Life Course," *Psychology and Aging* 30, no. 1 (2015): 120–135.

22. Berrin Erdogan et al., "Whistle While You Work: A Review of the Life Satisfaction Literature." *Journal of Management* 38, no. 4 (2012): 1039.

23. Bowling et al., "A Meta-Analysis of the Predictors," 601.

24. Strumpfer and de Bruin, "Antonovsky's Sense of Coherence," 1.

25. Strumpfer and de Bruin, "Antonovsky's Sense of Coherence," 1.

26. Bruk-Lee et al., "Replicating and Extending," 159.

Chapter 9

1. Career Igniter, "How Many Hours a Week Does a Lawyer Work?" accessed August 14, 2015, http://www.careerigniter.com/questions/how-many-hours-a-week-does-a-lawyer-work/.

2. CareerCast, "2015 Jobs Rated Methodology," accessed June 4, 2015, http://www.careeercast.com/jobs-rated/2015-jobs-rated-methodology.

3. CareerCast, "Jobs Rated Report 2015: Ranking the Top 200 Jobs," accessed June 11, 2015, http://www.careercast.com/jobs-rated/jobs-rated-report-2015-ranking-top-200-jobs.

4. CareerCast, "Jobs Rated 2011: Ranking 200 Jobs from Best to Worst," accessed June 11, 2015, http://www.careercast.com/jobs-rated/2011-ranking-200-jobs-best-worst;

CareerCast, "Jobs Rated 2012: Ranking 200 Jobs from Best to Worst," accessed June 12, 2015, http://www.careercast.com/jobs-rated/2012-ranking-200-jobs-best-worst; CareerCast, "Jobs Rated 2013: Ranking 200 Jobs from Best to Worst," accessed June 12, 2015, http://www.careercast.com/jobs-rated/best-jobs-2013; CareerCast, "Jobs Rated 2014: Ranking 200 Jobs from Best to Worst, accessed June 12, 2015, http://www.career cast.com/jobs-rated/jobs-rated-2014-ranking-200-jobs-best-worst.

5. *U.S. News and World Report*, "Best Careers 2011: Tips for Landing Our List," accessed August 17, 2015, http://money.usnews.com/money /careers/slideshows/best-careers-2011-tips-for-landing-jobs-on-our -list/2; *U.S. News and World Report*, "The Best Jobs of 2012," accessed June 13, 2015, http://money.usnews.com/money/careers/articles/2012/02/27 /the-best-jobs-of-2012; *U.S. News and World Report*, "The Best Jobs of 2013," accessed August 17, 2015," http://money.usnews.com/money /careers/articles/2012/12/18/the-best-jobs-of-2013?page=3; *U.S. News and World Report*, "The Best Jobs of 2014," accessed August 17, 2015," http://money.usnews.com/money/careers/articles/2014/01/23/the -best-jobs-of-2014?page=2; *U.S. News and World Report*, "The 100 Best Jobs," accessed June 13, 2015, http://money.usnews.com/careers /best-jobs/rankings/the-100-best-jobs.

6. CNNMoney, "Best Jobs in America," accessed June 13, 2015, http:// money.cnn.com/pf/best-jobs/2012/; CNNMoney, "Best Jobs in America," accessed June 13, 2015, http://money.cnn.com/pf/best-jobs/2013 /full_list/; CNNMoney, "Best Jobs in America," accessed August 3, 2015, http://money.cnn/pf/best-jobs/2015/list/.

7. CareerBliss, "CareerBliss Happiest and Unhappiest Jobs in America—2012," accessed June 12, 2015, http://www.careerbliss .com/facts-and-figures/happiest-and-unhappiest-jobs-17/; CareerBliss, "CareerBliss Happiest and Unhappiest Jobs in America—2013," accessed June 12, 2015, http://www.careerbliss.com/facts-and-figures /careerbliss-happiest-and-unhappiest-jobs-in-america-2013/; CareerBliss, "CareerBliss Happiest and Unhappiest Jobs in America—2015," accessed June 12, 2015, http://www.careerbliss.com/facts-and-figures /careerbliss-happiest-and-unhappiest-jobs-in-america-2015/; Forbes, "The 20 Happiest Jobs," accessed August 17, 2015, http://www.forbes .com/pictures/efkk45gmhl/the-20-happiest-jobs/; Forbes, "The Happiest and Unhappiest Jobs of 2014," accessed August 3, 2015, http://www .forbes.com/pictures/mkl45eeilm/the-happiest-and-unhappiest-jobs-in -america/.

8. Laurence Shatkin, *200 Best Jobs for Introverts* (St Paul: Jist Publishing, 2008); Laurence Shatkin, *Best Jobs for the 21st Century*, 6th

ed. (St Paul: Jist Publishing, 2012), 16; Laurence Shatkin, *300 Best Jobs without a Four-Year Degree*, 4th ed. (St Paul: Jist Publishing); Michael Farr and Laurence Shatkin, *200 Best Jobs for College Graduates*, 4th ed. (St Paul: Jist Publishing, 2009).

9. The top-10 best jobs for women from 2013 to 2015 and the top-10 happiest jobs for young professionals (2014) and college graduates (2015) can be found at http://nbaldwin.people.ua.edu/uploads/9/6/0/3/96039570/follower_appendices_chapt_9_web.pdf.

10. Forbes, "America's Most Prestigious Professions," accessed July 28, 2015, http://www.forbes.com/sites/niallmccarthy/2014/11/07/americas-most-prestigious-professions-infographic; CareerCast, "Jobs Rated Report 2015"; *U.S. News and World Report*, "The 100 Best Jobs"; CNNMoney, "Best Jobs in America," accessed August 3, 2015, http://money.cnn/pf/best-jobs/2015/list/.

Chapter 10

1. Bert Christensen, *Your Daily Moment of Zen*, accessed July 4, 2016, http://bertc.com/subfour/truth/momentzen.htm.

2. Katie D. Wolfe, "How to Manage a Micromanaging Boss," *Forbes*, April 11, 2013, accessed August 4, 2016, http://www.forbes.com/sites/dailymuse/2013/04/11/how-to-manage-a-micromanaging-boss/#2d18a1f32b67.

3. Amy Gallo, "Stop Being Micromanaged," *Harvard Business Review*, September 22, 2011, https://hbr.org/2011/09/stop-being-micromanaged.

4. Craig Dowden, "Micromanagement: Underlying Motivators and Proposed Solutions." *The Canadian Manager* (Spring 2012): 24–25, 2; Gallo, "Stop Being Micromanaged."

5. Amy Smith, "Managing Micromanagers," *Consulting—Specifying Engineer*, September 2013, http://www.csemag.com/single-article/managing-micromanagers/4f3d9c579ee78185050caf269377a234.html; Wolf, "How to Manage."

6. Wolf, "How to Manage."

7. Wolf, "How to Manage."

8. Susan Adams, "What to Do if Your Boss Is a Micromanager," *Forbes Leadership*, July, 3, 2014, http://www.forbes.com/sites/susanadams/2014/07/03/what-to-do-if-your-boss-is-a-micromanager/#10dcbe0a6971.

9. Gallo, "Stop Being Micromanaged."

10. Wolf, "How to Manage," 2.

11. Abraham H. Maslow, "A Theory of Human Motivation," *The Psychology of Science* 50, no. 4 (1943): 370–396.

12. Wolf, "How to Manage."

13. Gallo, "Stop Being Micromanaged."

14. Dowden, "Micromanagement"; Amy Smith, "Managing Micro-managers"; Gallo, "Stop Being Micromanaged"; Roy H. Lubit, *Coping with Toxic Managers, Subordinates, and Other Difficult People* (Upper Saddle River, NJ: Pearson Education, 2004); Jean-Francois Manzoni and Jean-Louis Barsoux, *The Set-Up-to-Fail Syndrome: How Good Managers Cause Good People to Fail* (Boston, MA: Harvard Business School Publishing, 2002).

15. Gallo, "Stop Being Micromanaged"; Manzoni and Barsoux, *The Set-Up-to-Fail.*

16. Lubit, *Coping with Toxic Managers*, 48.

17. Dowden, "Micromanagement"; Gallow, "Stop Being Micromanaged."

18. Adams, "What to Do if Your Boss Is a Micromanager"; Dowden, "Micromanagement"; Gallo, "Stop Being Micromanaged"; Lubit, *Coping with Toxic Managers*; Smith, "Managing Micromanagers."

19. Lubit, *Coping with Toxic Managers*, 48.

20. Walter Kiechel and Sarah Hammes, "Breaking Bad News to the Boss," *Fortune*, April 9, 1990, //archive.fortune.com/magazines/fortune/fortune_archive/1990/04/09/73349/index.htm.

21. Robert J. Bies, "The Delivery of Bad News in Organizations: A Framework for Analysis," *Journal of Management* 39, no. 1 (2013): 136–162.

22. Bies, "The Delivery of Bad News"; Robert J. Bies, "The 10 Commandments for Delivering Bad News," *Forbes Leadership Forum*, May 30, 2012, http://www.forbes.com/sites/forbesleadershipforum/2012/05/30/10-commandments-for-delivering-bad-news/#1cb191e61df9.

23. Jean-Francios Manzoni, "A Better Way to Deliver Bad News." *Harvard Business Review* 80, no. 9 (2002): 114–119.

24. Alan R. Dennis and Susan T. Kinney, "Testing Media Richness Theory in the New Media: The Effects, Cures, Feedback, and Task Equivocality," *Information Systems Research* 9 (1998): 256–274.

25. Bies, "The Delivery of Bad News"; Lew McCreary, "Winning Over Your New Boss," in *HBR Guide to Managing Up and Across*, ed. Harvard Business Review (Boston: Harvard Business Review, 2013).

26. Bies, "The Delivery of Bad News"; Kiechel and Hammes, "Breaking Bad News."

27. McCreary, "Winning Over Your New Boss."

28. Kiechel and Hammes, "Breaking Bad News"; Deb Bright, *The Truth Doesn't Have to Hurt* (New York: Amacom, 2014); Robert E. Clark and Emily E. Labeff, "Death Telling: Managing the Delivery of Bad News," *Journal of Health and Social Behavior* 23 (December 1982): 223–243.

29. Kerry Patterson et al., *Crucial Conversations: Tools for Talking When Stakes are High* (New York: McGraw-Hill, 2002).

30. Patterson et al., *Crucial Conversations*, 152.

31. Patterson et al., *Crucial Conversations*, 159, 202.

32. Amy M. Do, Alexander V. Rupert, and George Wolford, "Evaluation of Pleasurable Experiences. The Peak Rule," *Psychonomic Bulletin and Review* 15 (2008): 96–98; Angela M. Legg and Kate Sweeney, "Do You Want the Good News or Bad News First? The Nature and Consequences of News Order Preferences," *Personality and Social Psychology Bulletin* 40, no. 3 (2014): 279–288; William T. Ross and Itamar Simonson, "Evaluations of Pairs of Experiences: A Preference for a Happy Ending," *Journal of Behavioral Decision Making* 4, no. 4 (1991): 273–282.

33. Legg and Sweeney, "Do You Want the Good News."

34. Bill J. Harrison, "Confronting the Unethical Boss: Advice for Fundraising Professionals," *Nonprofit World* 24, no. 5 (2006): 8–10.

35. Robert Half, "The Boss Is Unethical. What Should I Do?" *Management Accounting* 75, no. 1 (1993): f.

36. Mary Uhl-Bien and Melisa K. Carsten, "Being Ethical When the Boss Is Not," *Organization Dynamics* 36, no. 2 (2007):187–201.

37. Richard P. Nielsen, "Changing Unethical Organization Behavior," *The Academy of Management Executive* 3, no. 2 (1989): 123–130.

38. Harrison, "Confronting the Unethical Boss."

39. Nielsen, "Changing Unethical Organization"; Uhl-Bien and Carsten, "Being Ethical."

40. Half, "The Boss Is Unethical."

41. Harrison, "Confronting the Unethical Boss."

42. Uhl-Bien and Carsten, "Being Ethical."

Chapter 11

1. The content of Table 11.1 is from the following sources: Innocent Echiejile, "Dealing with Sexual Harassment," *Employee Counseling Today* 5, no. 4 (1993): 21–29; EEOC, "Policy Guidance on Current Issues of Sexual Harassment" (March 19, 1990): 1–13; EEOC, "Sexual Harassment," accessed July 10, 2016, https://www.eeoc.gov/laws/types/sexual_harassment.cfm; Elizabeth Smolensky and Brian H. Kleiner, "How to Prevent Sexual Harassment in the Workplace," *Equal Opportunity International* 22, no. 2 (2003): 59–66; Deidre Takeyama and Brian H. Kleiner, "How to Prevent Sexual Harassment in the Workplace," *Equal Opportunity International* 17, no. 6 (1998): 6–12.

2. "Examples of Sexual Harassment," accessed July 8, 2016, http://burro.cwru.edu/women/harassment/examples.html.

3. MSPB, *Sexual Harassment in the Federal Workplace* (Washington, DC: U.S. MSPB, 1995).

4. EEOC, "Employer Liability for Harassment," accessed July 10, 2016, https://www.eeoc.gov/laws/types/harassment.cfm.

5. EEOC, "Sexual Harassment," accessed July 10, 2016, https://www.eeoc.gov/laws/types/harassment.cfm.

6. In determining welcomeness, the EEOC considers, on a case by case basis, the "record as a whole and totality of circumstances," as well as "whether the victims conduct is consistent or inconsistent with assertions that the sexual conduct is unwelcome." EEOC, "Policy Guidance," 5.

7. Wayne L. Anderson and Andre Bouravnev, "Sexual Harassment: The Good, the Bad, and the Ugly," *Franklin Business and Law* 11, no. 4 (2011): 31.

8. EEOC, "Policy Guidance," 6.

9. EEOC, "Policy Guidance," 5.

10. EEOC, "Policy Guidance," 7.

11. EEOC, "Policy Guidance," 9.

12. EEOC, "Policy Guidance," 10.

13. Reeves v. C.H. Robinson Worldwide, Inc. No. 07-10270 (11th Cir. Jan. 20, 2010).

14. Jeanne D. Maes and Robert A. Shearer, "Dealing with Sexual Harassment in the Workplace: Collaborating Throughout the Organization to Produce Policies that Motivate," *Equal Opportunity International* 16, no. 1 (1997): 1–7.

15. Thomas L. Tang, and Stacie L. McCollum, "Sexual Harassment in the Workplace," *Public Personnel Management* 25, no. 1 (1996): 53–58.

16. Anderson and Bouravnev, "Sexual Harassment."

17. Brieana D. Roumeliotis and Brian H. Kleiner, "Individual Response Strategies to Sexual Harassment," *Equal Opportunity International* 24, no. 5/6 (2005): 41–48.

18. Martha E. Eller, "Sexual Harassment: Prevention, Not Protection," *Restaurant Administration Quarterly* 30, no. 4 (1990): 84–89.

19. Eller, "Sexual Harassment," 89; Roumeliotis and Kleiner, "Individual Response Strategies"; Tang and McCollum, "Sexual Harassment in the Workplace."

20. Eller, "Sexual Harassment"; Roumeliotis and Kleiner, "Individual Response Strategies"; Tang and McCollum, "Sexual Harassment in the Workplace."

21. Bureau of National Affairs, *Preventing Sexual Harassment: A Fact Sheet for Employees* (Washington, DC: Bureau of National Affairs, 1997).

22. Bureau of National Affairs, *Preventing Sexual Harassment*, 1997.

23. Findings also include an "other" option preferred by women as the number one option in the 1988 study. MSPB, *Sexual Harassment*.

24. MSPB, *Sexual Harassment*, 30.

25. Roy H. Lubit, *Coping with Toxic Managers, Subordinates, and Other Difficult People* (Upper Saddle River, NJ: Pearson Education, 2004), 138–139.

26. Gina G. Scott, *The Survival Guide for Dealing with Bad Bosses* (New York: Amacom, 2006).

27. Gonzague Dufour, *Managing Your Manager: How to Get Ahead with Any Type of Boss* (New York: McGraw Hill, 2011).

28. Lubit, *Coping with Toxic Managers*, 106, 115.

29. Dufour, *Managing Your Manager*, 13.

30. Dufour, *Managing Your Manager*, 18.

31. Dufour, *Managing Your Manager*, 19.

32. Scott, *The Survival Guide*.

33. Lubit, *Coping with Toxic Managers*.

34. Smith, "Managing Micromanagers"; Lubit, *Coping with Toxic Managers*.

35. Amit K. Nandkeolyar et al., "Surviving an Abusive Supervisor: The Joint Roles of Conscientiousness and Coping Strategies," *Journal of Applied Psychology* 99, no. 1 (2014): 138.

36. Lubit, *Coping with Toxic Managers*, 115.

Chapter 12

1. "Mike Bobo," *Georgiadogs.com Home of Georgia Athletics*, accessed August 24, 2015, http://www.georgiadogs.com/sports/m-footbl/mtt/bobo_mike00.html.

2. Sports Reference/College Football, "Players: Mike Bobo," http://www.sports-reference.com/cfb/players/mike-bobo-2.html.

3. Sports Reference/College Football, "Players: Mike Bobo."

4. Hines was a four-time National Football League (NFL) Pro Bowler, the MVP of Super Bowl XL, and the 2011 winner of *Dancing with the Stars*. Robert was the first-round draft pick of the New England Patriots and a Pro-Bowler his rookie season before sustaining an injury that almost required the amputation of his leg.

5. R. Michael Bobo, in discussion with the author, July 2016.

6. Champ became a 12-time NFL Pro-Bowler who will, undoubtedly, be inducted into the NFL Hall of Fame someday.

7. Sports Reference/College Football, "Players: Mike Bobo."

8. Barbara Kellerman, *Followership: How Followers Are Creating Change and Changing Leaders* (Boston, MA: Harvard Business Review Press, 2008).

9. Gilley Pressley, in discussion with the author, June 2016.

10. Susan Barfoot, in discussion with the author, June 2016.

11. Susan Dooley, in discussion with the author, June 2016.

12. Extra Special People, accessed September 5, 2015, http://extraspecial people.com/.

Index

About the Author

J. NORMAN BALDWIN is professor of political science at the University of Alabama, where he has served as director of Graduate Programs, Undergraduate Programs, and the Master of Public Administration Program. He teaches courses on how to organize and manage employees in public service and conducts research on followership, diversifying organizations, whistle-blowing, economic development, and differences between public and private organizations. Arguably UA's most highly honored faculty member of the 21st century, Baldwin is the recipient of the Morris Mayer Award, Buford Peace Award, Other Club Person of the Year Award, Outstanding Commitment to Students Award, Service Project of the Year Award, the Samuel S. May Award, and the Algernon Sydney Sullivan Award. Outside of work, he performs the lead vocals in a band and supports Alabama Arise, Amnesty International, the International Justice Mission, Refugees International, the Children's Hunger Fund, and the Center for Victims Against Torture.